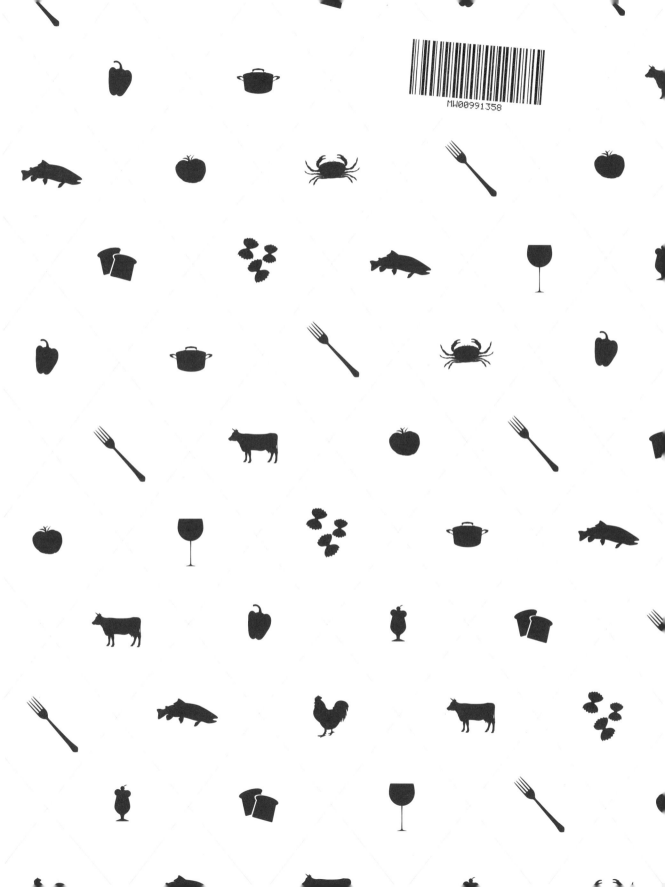

MW00991358

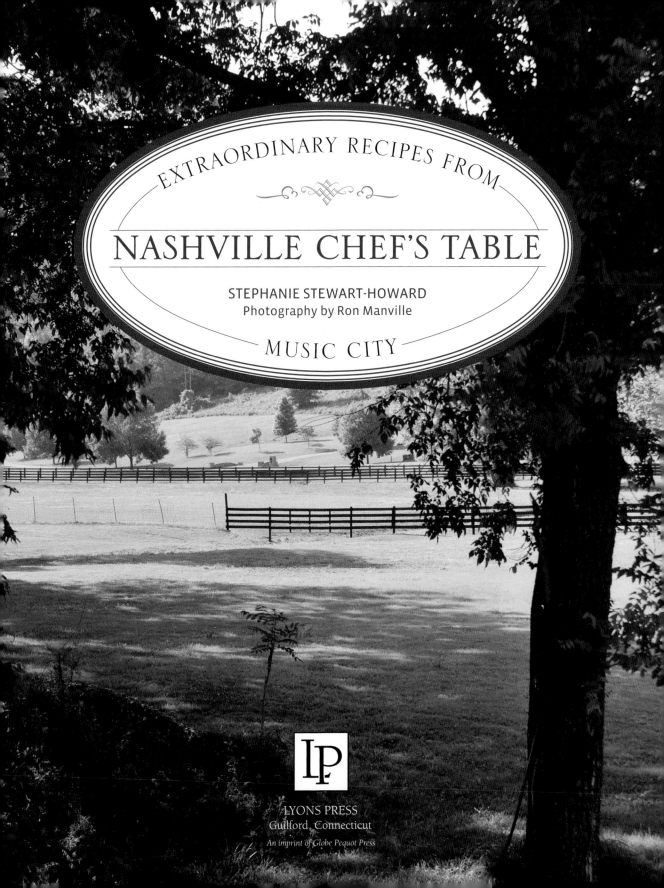

EXTRAORDINARY RECIPES FROM

NASHVILLE CHEF'S TABLE

STEPHANIE STEWART-HOWARD
Photography by Ron Manville

MUSIC CITY

LP

LYONS PRESS
Guilford, Connecticut
An imprint of Globe Pequot Press

To buy books in quantity for corporate use
or incentives, call **(800) 962–0973**
or e-mail **premiums@GlobePequot.com.**

Lyons Press is an imprint of Globe Pequot Press.

All photography by Ron Manville

Editor: Amy Lyons
Project Editor: Julie Marsh
Text Design: Libby Kingsbury
Layout Artist: Nancy Freeborn

Library of Congress Cataloging-in-Publication Data is on file.

ISBN 978-0-7627-9220-7

Printed in the United States of America

10 9 8 7 6 5 4 3 2 1

Restaurants and chefs often come and go, and menus are ever-changing. We recommend you call ahead to obtain current information before visiting any of the establishments in this book.

This book is dedicated to my husband Seth Howard, for all the love and support he's given to me, and to my late grandmothers, Myra Stewart and Lula Webb, who introduced me to the art of Southern food.

Contents

ACKNOWLEDGMENTS xi

INTRODUCTION xiii

AM@FM 1
Edamame Salsa

Arnold's Country Kitchen .2
Catfish
Southern Green Beans
Mac & Cheese
Tomato Basil Pie

The Bang Candy Company 10
Raspberry Lemon Cloud 9

Bella Nashville 13
Brussels Sprouts & Bacon Pizza

Biscuit Love Truck 18
The Princess Biscuit

BLVD Nashville 21
Brussels Sprouts

Burger Up 24
The Ramsey Burger

Cabana Restaurant 26
Crab Cakes with Asian Slaw & Mango Chili Sauce
Lobster & Brie "Mac and Cheese" with Benton's Smoky Mountain Country Ham Crisp

Caffe Nonna 30
Smoked Salmon with Orecchiette Pasta

CAPITOL GRILLE..34
Hanger Steak with Vegetable Frites & Double-Fried French Fries
Spring Trout
Blueberry Cobbler Cocktail

CITY HOUSE 42
Porch Pounder

THE COCOA TREE...45
Amy's Balsamic Raspberry Truffles
Sofia's Sweet Potato Truffles

CORK & COW 48
Butternut Rotolo
Green Means Go
Cascade Cooler

DOZEN BAKERY..52
Brown Sugar Shortcakes

1808 GRILLE...55
Pork Tenderloin with Peach Salad, Shaved Radicchio & Sweet Cherry Gastrique
Tennessee Julep
West End Julep

8TH AND ROAST 59
Vanilla Bean Café Au Lait
Mini Spinach Feta Frittata

ETCH..62
Etch Duck Breast with Ginger Grits, Sweet Potato Guava Schmear, Cranberry Relish & Pear Butter
Tuna, Eggplant & Spinach Ponzu Salad
Flourless Chocolate Cake with Coffee Crème Brûlée, Milk Chocolate Crumble & Mocha Mousse
Whisper Creek Wakeup Chiller

FIDO 72
The PC Muffin

55 SOUTH 74
Nashville Hot Chicken

FIREPOT CHAI 78
The Cauveri Cocktail
Firepot Chai Hot Toddy
Chai Fried Chicken

FLYTE WORLD DINING AND WINE 82
Pig Ears with Waffles

F. SCOTT'S RESTAURANT & JAZZ BAR 85
Sweet Potato Gnocchi with Spiced Parmesan Cream

THE GRILLED CHEESERIE GOURMET GRILLED CHEESE TRUCK 88
Grilled Cheese
Old-Fashioned Tomato Soup

HOLLAND HOUSE BAR AND REFUGE 92
Listless Ease

JASMINE 94
Cucumber Salad

LOCKELAND TABLE, A COMMUNITY KITCHEN AND BAR 97
Southern Corn Bread
Collard Greens

THE LOVELESS CAFÉ 100
Carrot Pudding
Goo Goo Cluster Pie

MANGIA NASHVILLE 106
Penne with Porcini Cognac Cream Sauce
Zeppole

MARCHÉ 110
Salad with Fresh Strawberries, Blue Cheese, Toasted Almonds & White Balsamic Vinaigrette

MARGOT CAFE 113
Chicken with Fresh Spring Peas, Potatoes, Lemon & Mint

MARTIN'S BAR-B-QUE JOINT 116
Redneck Taco

MAS TACOS POR FAVOR 119
Chicken Tortilla Soup

MASON'S AND MASON BAR 122
Beef Tartare with Pecan Romesco

MERCHANTS RESTAURANT 125
Strawberry Salad
Johnny Cash's "Old Iron Pot" Family-Style Chili

MIDTOWN CAFE 130
Smoked Salmon Dressing

MISS DAISY'S AT GRASSLAND MARKET 132
Pecan Cheese Wafers
Miss Daisy's Hot Artichoke Dip
Miss Daisy's Black Bean Salad

THE PATTERSON HOUSE 136
Duck Hunter

PROVENCE BREADS & CAFE 138
French Baguettes
Creamy Tomato Basil Soup

PUCKETT'S RESTAURANT & GROCERY 143
Puckett's Chicken Salad
Puckett's King's French Toast

RED PONY 147
Braised Pork Shanks with Red Wine Jus

RUMOURS 12TH AND DIVISION 150
No. 1104
Char Siu Meatballs

SAFFIRE 156
Mac & Cheese
Chicken Fried Chicken

SILLY GOOSE..160
King Kong Couscous

SLOCO..163
Pulled Pork with Caraway Slaw & Homemade Dijon Mustard

THE SOUTHERN STEAK & OYSTER..............................167
BBQ Shrimp
My Way (Pasta)

SUNSET GRILL...172
Beets & Heat Salad
Shrimp & Grits with Pickled Okra
Jack Daniel's Pecan Pie

SWAGRUHA...178
Vegetable Korma

TABLE 3 RESTAURANT & MARKET.............................182
Bouillabaisse
Onion Soup Gratinée

TAVERN..188
Thai Cobb Salad

WHISKEY KITCHEN..190
Chipotle Mac & Cheese

THE YELLOW PORCH..192
Tennessee Sharp Cheddar Cheese Fritters
Chow Chow

RESOURCE GUIDE..197

INDEX..200

ABOUT THE AUTHOR & PHOTOGRAPHER........................206

THE SECOND FIDDLE
MUSIC
HONKY TONK
CITY
WELCOME TO
LAYLA'S
NASHVILLE
2013 CMA MUSIC FESTIVAL
FAN FAIR Flashbacks
CMAFEST.COM
Second Fiddle
ATM
BAR-B-Q
HILL BILLY GRILL
HONKY TONK GRILL

Acknowledgments

Trying to represent Nashville's burgeoning food culture in such a small space has been a stunning task. I owe a lot of gratitude to the people who taught me what food and food writing are all about in this spectacular town.

The marvelous Martha Stamps familiarized me in so many ways with Nashville's traditional food culture, and food critic Kay West introduced me to both the newest and the oldest of the restaurants that define who we are as a culinary city. Miss Daisy King reminds me what Nashville cooking is truly all about with everything she does.

My friends and fellow writers Chris Chamberlain, Jennifer Justus, Dara Carson, Kay West, and Tammy Algood have inspired me, as have the chefs and artists who have become more than passing acquaintances, including Pat Martin, Tyler Brown, Jason McConnell, Carl Schultheis, Tandy Wilson, Siva Pavuluri, Sarah Souther, James Hensley, and Sarah Scarborough. Marne Duke, Robin Riddell Jones, Janet Kurtz,and Jennifer Hagan-Dier, thanks for your knowledge and advice over the years.

Photographer Ron Manville and I have worked together quite a bit over the past few years, first at Nashville Lifestyles, then on other projects. He has taught me to look at images of food in a way I never thought possible, and I'm delighted to have had the chance to work with him on this book.

My parents, Joe and Yvonne Stewart, opened up the culinary world for me, not only from their own Southern background, but through world travel and the opportunity to experience native foods across the globe—and they taught me to bring the recipes home and cook them for myself. They are both outstanding cooks, and I'm lucky they still believe in family meals.

Likewise, my late grandmothers, Myra Fendley Stewart and Lula Prillaman Webb, were my first teachers about eating fresh food you grew yourself and just how good the simplest things, like biscuits and yeast rolls, could be. (Needless to say, they were also both absolute masters of the complex, especially when it came to dessert.)

The greatest thanks of all belong to my husband, Seth Howard, who encouraged me to pursue my dreams and put up with my incessant talk about this book. He is my constant source of inspiration in all the arts I pursue and the goals that I make for myself.

Introduction

Nashville has been a music town for decades now, ever since the Grand Ole Opry began in the 1930s with the rise of "old-time" music, followed by an even greater musical influx after World War II, with the birth of Music Row. It dates back to the days of RCA Studio B, on to Hank and Patsy, through George and Tammy and Dolly and Porter, then Willie and Kris and Johnny and Merle, on to Garth Brooks and George Strait, to Carrie Underwood and Blake Shelton. We've been viewed through the eyes of *Hee Haw* and Robert Altman's *Nashville* and *Nashville* the TV show. But there is more to "Music City" than years of music—then and now.

Two thousand thirteen, the year this book was written, saw Nashville become an "it" city in the eyes of the nation and the world—about, for once, more than just the musical superstars. Dozens of publications, domestic and international, rushed to talk about us— our food, our arts, our craftspersons, our businesses, our sports, and our real estate— and proclaim us the hottest thing in the nation.

Well, that's nice and all, but most of those things were here prior to this year, and more will happen when the fickle media has moved on to Cleveland, Syracuse, or Billings. The eyes of the world will still be on us, because we genuinely have that much to offer, even if we aren't the "hot new thing."

In this moment, as the world rediscovers us, our culinary culture is blooming. Unlike Charleston and New Orleans, we don't have a fundamentally defined cuisine that's spent two hundred years fermenting into something distinct. We have instead a food history that is deeply tied to the history of the South itself.

Nashville, and the areas surrounding it in Davidson, Williamson, and Rutherford Counties, had a thriving Native American culture for centuries before European settlers arrived. In 1779 James Robertson and John Donelson left North Carolina and set up Fort Nashborough, a replica of which can still be visited today. The presence of the Cumberland and Harpeth Rivers provided myriad advantages, from irrigation for cotton fields to river transport, and a city was born.

The nineteenth century offered up notable pieces of American history, from presidents Andrew Jackson, James K. Polk, and Andrew Johnson to Civil War battles and occupation. After the Civil War, Nashville grew up as a center of trade, thanks to the railroads. If it had any national culinary claim to fame prior to World War II, it was probably the celebrated coffee blend at the Maxwell House Hotel downtown.

As one of my local culinary heroines, Miss Daisy King, tells it, until comparatively recently there was no defined restaurant history in Nashville. What you got when you visited the city were a lot of chain-type places, with a few notable local spots—many more renowned for the songwriters who hung out there than for the food served. All the big department stores, like downtown's late, lamented Cain-Sloan, had their own in-house restaurants, and a few places, like Sperry's and Jimmy Kelly's (both steak houses), managed to make names for themselves as fine-dining institutions by the 1970s (Kelly's dates to 1934).

Miss Daisy's own famous tearoom got its start in Franklin (just to the south of Nashville proper) in 1974 and helped define the moment's "taste" of Nashville. During the 1980s locally owned places finally started to gain a slender foothold, though most were downtown or in Green Hills, not spread out in the smaller neighborhoods—unless you counted small iconic places like Bobby's Dairy Dip in Sylvan Park.

When my parents moved here in the mid-1990s (I was in grad school), the chains still dominated. A handful of really good locally owned places had sprung up by then—F. Scott's, Jay Pennington's Bound'ry, and Randy Rayburn's Sunset Grill among them—and the owners of these and other locations banded together to form Nashville Originals, an organization to promote and support independent restaurant owners in and around the city. That organization still thrives today, supporting Nashville Restaurant Week and providing deals to patrons who come out and explore locally owned eateries.

I jumped in and out of the city until about 2004, when I settled here permanently and reinvented myself from theater professional to journalist. Over the past nearly ten years, the restaurant scene has changed uncannily fast. Talented chefs, many trained under culinary experts at our own longer-standing originals, are branching out and starting their own places, and new chefs are moving to town to start their careers here, rather than choosing larger, more trafficked locations.

Neighborhood restaurants are cropping up—not with the aim of being giant powerhouses, but intending to serve very good food of all types to people who live nearby and help build neighborhood cultures. Germantown, Sylvan Park, East Nashville, and even longtime holdout and chain-centric Franklin are now thriving with those new establishments—places that, in the words of local supper club creator and chef Avon Lyons, "are manageable, with delicious food. They're focused on sharing with just enough people, not trying to bring in massive crowds and not spending the budget on public relations."

We find these restaurants everywhere now, from the older and more established, like East Nashville's Margot Cafe, to Jason McConnell's more recent Red Pony in Franklin or Germantown's brand-new Rolf and Daughters. Even the exceptional "old-school" spots, like Capitol Grille in the Hermitage Hotel, attain that feel, thanks to the work of their chefs and dedicated staffs. We tend to favor intimacy over the overblown and outsized.

With our growing interest in fresh foods and the spread of the Slow Food movement and others concepts like it, we've built an exceptional system of farmers' markets, with one accessible to nearly everyone, regardless of where you live in the city, and a huge and thriving downtown Nashville Farmers' Market. These markets not only help us support local farms and make fresh produce more readily available, but also encourage and support up-and-coming chefs, restaurateurs, and artisan food producers.

Nashville has moved from a place where a few restaurants had microbrew options to thriving microbreweries all over the city—Yazoo, Jackalope, Blackstone, Bosco's, Mayday (in nearby Murfreesboro), Fat Bottom, Cool Springs, and more—some of which are gaining serious national attention. A change in our state laws has made Tennessee's microdistilleries, many centered in and around the Nashville area (Speakeasy, Corsair, Collier & McKeel), something to be talked about on a worldwide level. And each May the Toast to Tennessee Wine Festival comes to town, showcasing the state's thirty-some

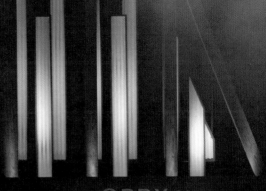

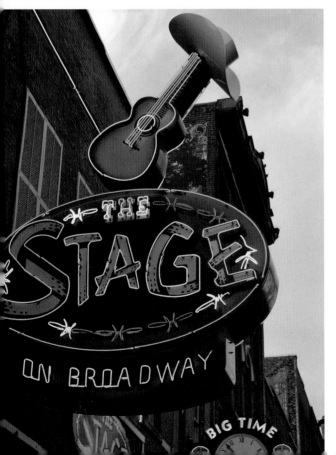

wineries and underlining that places like Château Ross, Beachhaven, and Arrington Vineyards are making things that aren't the syrupy wine equivalent of overly sweet tea.

In the past few years, we've evolved further still: Scott Witherow's Olive & Sinclair chocolate company and Sarah Scarborough's Firepot Chai make a good representation of the plethora of small, artisan food businesses that have emerged, impacted our food landscape, and moved to national prominence.

Amidst all this growth, our chefs have become the backbone of the rising trend of the farm-to-fork movement that's still growing forty years after Alice Waters popularized the idea. More, they're reintroducing us to the things that are best about Southern food. What was once intrinsic to the Nashville and Southeastern diet is being rediscovered.

So what is Tennessee food, anyway? Like most of the cuisine native to the South, it depends on seasonal eating and what's available on the farm at the time. It is the food of farmers more than it is the culinary creation of the affluent, and like much of what we love best about classic French or Italian country cuisine, it grows out of a need to make the best possible with what one has at hand.

At its heart, traditional Southern food is tied to the food our grandparents ate growing up during the Depression, which isn't all that different from what their own parents and grandparents ate during their farm-based childhoods. Many of us who are adults now are fortunate enough to have had grandparents and great-grandparents who still maintained "gardens" (my grandparents essentially had small farms in town) through our childhoods, who canned the fresh produce or froze it and sent it home in boxes with us each time we visited.

What you got was straightforward: corn and beans, peppers, greens, squashes, and pumpkins; tomatoes whole and made into sauces; chow chows and pickles, and even old-style fermented sauerkrauts. Jellies and jams and preserves were there, too, made

from the fruit they or the neighbors grew. Today we connect all of that with the notion of farm-to-fork and somehow often forget that it's a rediscovery, not a new thing.

Coming from a Southern family (Virginia and South Carolina, in full disclosure), albeit one centered first in the military, then corporate America, I learned about this kind of food from my own parents and grandparents. The first thing I learned to cook was biscuits, by the time I was about six years old. Self-rising flour, shortening, milk—even a kid could do it, and knead dough, and make a good biscuit. To this day I can make them without ever resorting to a measuring cup and still get it right. Thanks, Mom.

My friends are learning how to can again, and make jams and preserves. Dara Carson, who has a farm of her own as well as a little house "in town," is my constant inspiration in this. We're learning to forage—flowers like honeysuckle for simple syrups, wild berries and herbs, morels. In part we're learning it because it's on trend, no doubt about that. But in a few years it may not be, and we will still have the skill. We've learned to appreciate the taste of things that don't come from supermarket shelves—that are fresh, or freshly preserved—and value that which we make with our own hands.

Many of us are buying chicken, pork, or beef directly from the farmers. There is new appreciation for game meats like wild turkey, duck, and venison, and freshly caught fish that we can fry up in cornmeal or grill. Barbecue is a thing for us—slow-cooking meats until they are tender to falling apart, then shredding them with a good fork.

And with that, as we follow the trends, we've returned to the Southern foodways of previous generations. Into it we've blended the popular post–World War II starches, like macaroni and cheese, and made them our own with willful delight.

When we prepare these simple, fresh foods, cooking them in a traditional manner— the turnip greens long simmered with a bit of pork, the tomatoes and cucumbers marinated overnight in vinegar and oil—we return to our roots.

Nashville's chef contingent is very aware of this past, and true to it. A few of them, most notably Tyler Brown at Capitol Grille and Matt Lackey at Flyte, have turned farmer themselves. That doesn't mean that they aren't also blending in the tastes and traditions of other cultures—hints of South Asia and France, Germany and Morocco. They are indeed.

In point of fact, we have grown to enjoy ethnic food as a city in a way we never have before. But what seems to underlie the best of all of it now is the understanding that the shared past of fresh food and seasonal flavors—in our Southern culture and in others— produces the best meals. And it is the root of all our flavorful cooking.

When putting together this cookbook, I was faced with the daunting task of sorting out the most representative of Nashville's restaurant scene. My preliminary list had over a hundred places on it, and I've reduced it to half that for you here. I hope it will serve not only as a cookbook, but also as a guide to all Nashville has to offer, whether you're cooking for your family or planning a trip to the area.

As I wrote this book, Chef Sean Brock was preparing to open a Nashville version of his Charleston-favorite Husk, and several other chefs I knew were making announcements about new places and spaces across the city. I can only imagine that things will grow more exciting and expansive in the coming years, whether we are an "it" city of the moment or not.

AM@FM

900 Rosa L. Parks Boulevard, Germantown
(615) 291-4585
www.amfmnashville.com/
Chef/Owner: Arnold Myint

The simplicity and grace of Chef Arnold Myint's AM@FM (psst—that's Arnold Myint at the farmers' market) quickly made it one of my favorites at the downtown farmers' market when it appeared a couple of years ago. Open daily 11 a.m. to 5 p.m., AM@FM keeps generally longer hours than many of its market counterparts, but the timing is not its only appeal.

Arriving at the bright counter, you'll find a selection of sandwiches (I adore the Mu Shu Chicken wrap) suited to almost any dietary need, together with potential side offerings—usually salads and fresh vegetables in creative yet simple incarnations. A board lists the daily specials, including full-sized salads and soups. A rarity in the farmers' market, a wine list that offers a rather more in-depth set of options than simply red or white makes this a great late afternoon meeting spot as well. Of course, you expect the best from former *Top Chef* contestant Myint—he has proved himself again and again in this city.

The downtown farmers' market has done its best to bring in truly exceptional offerings to create an alternative to chains and drive-thrus for the business crowd downtown. AM@FM is one of the best examples of fresh, healthy, often locally sourced food being done right at a comparable cost. It meets the needs of those who want something with a hint of sophistication, but the menu options are diverse enough to have something to please everyone. A waiting line at lunch has customers dressed in everything from business suits to workmen's coveralls. And that's as it should be.

Edamame Salsa

(SERVES 4–6)

⅓ cup light soy sauce

⅓ cup rice vinegar

¼ cup olive oil

1 tablespoon sesame oil

1 cup granulated sugar

1 tablespoon Dijon mustard

2 cups shelled edamame (out of pods)

1 cup diced sweet white onion

1 cup diced tomato

½ cup sliced scallion

½ cup rough-chopped cilantro

2 tablespoons black and white sesame seeds

Whisk the soy sauce, vinegar, olive oil, sesame oil, sugar, and mustard together until sugar is dissolved.

Combine all the remaining ingredients in a mixing bowl. Add the dressing and store in the refrigerator until ready to serve.

ARNOLD'S COUNTRY KITCHEN

605 8TH AVENUE SOUTH, THE GULCH
(615) 256-4455
FACEBOOK.COM/ARNOLDSMEATAND3
CHEF: KAHLIL ARNOLD

The mythic meat-'n-three restaurant that dominates the Southern landscape gets taken to the next level with Arnold's Country Kitchen. It's not just the James Beard Foundation America's Classic Award or Guy Fieri's *Diners, Drive-Ins and Dives* that make that definitive, but the locals who line up daily from the moment the doors unlock. Set just at the boundary of The Gulch on 8th Avenue South, Arnold's has been a legend since Jack Arnold and his wife, Rose, started the whole thing thirty years ago. The chef these days is Jack's gifted son Kahlil, who astounds me both with his graciousness and his talent every time I walk in the place.

You never know just exactly what will turn up on the menu, though a board advertises the entrees by day of the week. The tiny space is always filled for lunch (no dinners, sorry), and you should expect to share a table if you and your party don't fill it up (there are plenty of two-tops).

When I go in, I have to admit a weakness for the roast beef, which Arnold's legends are made of, but there's also the fried chicken, the pork, the meat loaf—oh, man, the meat loaf. But meat-'n-three culture prides itself on doing traditional Southern foods right, and the catfish served up by Kahlil Arnold and his folks is meant to be enjoyed. If you're not catching them yourself, your grocery store or fishmonger should have them, even if you live in a non-catfish-centric part of the nation.

CATFISH

(SERVES 4–6)

5–6 (5–7 ounces each) farm-raised catfish fillets

8 cups warm water

3 tablespoons kosher salt

3 tablespoons hot sauce
   (Louisiana Hot Sauce preferred)

3 cups enriched, self-rising white cornmeal
   (White Lily preferred)

2 teaspoons salt

2 teaspoons black pepper

2 teaspoons granulated garlic

1 teaspoon cayenne pepper

6–8 cups canola oil

To brine the catfish, fill a bowl with warm water (hot tap water is fine) and whisk in kosher salt and hot sauce until salt evaporates. Put mixture in the freezer for 15–20 minutes. Remove from freezer and put catfish fillets in brine. (I usually put some ice cubes on top to keep the fish really cold.) Put in the fridge for about 3 hours or overnight.

When the fish is ready to be fried, mix the cornmeal, salt, pepper, garlic, and cayenne pepper in a bowl.

Remove catfish from fridge. Drain and rinse off brine in with cold water in a colander. Let excess water drain completely off.

Heat canola oil in a deep-dish sauté pan or iron skillet, making sure you don't put too much oil in it. You want to fill it a little less than halfway. Check the temperature with an oil thermometer. When the oil gets to 335°F, it's ready to go and you can turn it down a little.

Dredge both sides of the catfish in the cornmeal mixture. Shake off excess meal. Place the catfish in the skillet and cook for 5–6 minutes. Turn catfish over halfway with metal tongs during cooking if needed to get both sides browned.

Remove fish and set on a plate lined with paper towels so excess oil can drain. After about 15 seconds, it's ready to serve.

THE THREES

Khalil Arnold's Southern Green Beans, Mac & Cheese, and Tomato Basil Pie all complement the catfish recipe above. There are plenty of entrees you can pair them with, of course, but the trio together is fairly marvelous—hence the "meat-'n-three" concept. And all of them meet the "kid food" challenge when you're cooking for family.

These days, after a shift away from fresh foods over the past few decades, local produce, fresh and grown nearby, is making a comeback. Kahlil's mom, Rose, once told me that much of hers came from early-morning visits to the Nashville Farmers' Market. Once you taste them, it's easy to believe the Arnolds don't take fresh for granted.

The whole advantage to meat-'n-three style is that you get to choose from a wide variety to make up your plate.

SOUTHERN GREEN BEANS

(SERVES 8–10)

4 slices applewood smoked bacon, chopped

1 medium onion, chopped

1 tablespoon canola oil

2 pounds fresh-cut green beans

Pinch of crushed red pepper

6–8 cups chicken broth

Salt and freshly ground black pepper to taste

In a medium-size pot on medium-high heat, sauté the bacon for 5 minutes, stirring with a wooden spoon until browned.

Add onions and canola oil and stir for 3 minutes, until onions start looking translucent.

Add green beans, red pepper, and chicken broth and cook on same heat until half of the broth has evaporated, stirring every few minutes. It should take around 30 minutes. The longer you cook, the more flavor the green beans will absorb. Add water if needed.

Reduce heat to low and taste. Add salt and pepper if needed.

MAC & CHEESE

(SERVES 6–8)

Ask anyone what their favorite comfort food is, and if mac and cheese isn't on the list, they're probably lying. There are several variations on the genre in this book, but this one is fairly easy and really delicious.

8 cups water

2 tablespoons canola oil

2 cups macaroni noodles

2 tablespoons margarine

2 tablespoons flour

2 cups milk

2½ cups shredded American cheese, divided

1 teaspoon black pepper

1 teaspoon ground mustard seed

2 tablespoons grated Parmesan cheese

Pinch of salt

Paprika

In a medium pot, bring water to a boil. Add canola oil and noodles. Cook for 20 minutes, or until noodles swell and are soft. Drain in a colander.

Meanwhile, preheat oven to 325°F.

In a double boiler, melt margarine. When melted, stir in flour and cook for a few minutes until browned. Slowly add milk, whisking vigorously.

Add 2 cups of shredded cheese and stir until melted. Whisk in black pepper, mustard, and Parmesan cheese. Taste to see if a pinch of salt is needed.

In a small casserole dish, add noodles and stir in cheese sauce. Sprinkle ½ cup of shredded cheese on top. Lightly sprinkle paprika on top.

Put in preheated oven and cook for 30 minutes, or until cheese is bubbling around edges.

Tomato Basil Pie

(SERVES 6–8)

Tomato Basil Pie also touches on the Southern love for dairy products, even though the artisan cheese movement is a new thing for us. Both mac and cheese and this pie manage to make it to the top of the comfort food list, with their insistence on creamy cheeses.

4 medium fresh local tomatoes
1 9-inch frozen pie shell
3 tablespoons Cavender's All Purpose Greek
    Seasoning or to taste (available in most
    grocery store spice and seasoning aisles
    or from www.lacrawfish.com)
1 cup chopped fresh basil
¾ cup mayonnaise
3 cups shredded mild cheddar cheese

First, wash and core the tomatoes. Thinly slice the tomatoes and put on a plate lined with paper towels. You should have at least 3 layers and make sure there are paper towels between each layer. Refrigerate for at least 3 hours to let some of the juice from the tomatoes drain so the pie is not soggy.

Prebake pie shell for 30 minutes at 325°F. To keep the bottom from puffing, you should line the bottom crust with parchment paper and fill it with dried beans. After prebaking the crust and letting it cool, remove the beans and parchment paper.

Next, remove the tomatoes from the fridge. Cover the bottom of the piecrust with a layer of tomatoes. Shake the Cavender's on the layer of tomatoes and sprinkle some basil on them. Repeat the process for the next two layers.

In a separate mixing bowl, mix the mayo and cheese into a paste with a spatula. Put the cheese mixture on the top of the pie, smoothing it out with the spatula. Bake for 30–45 minutes or until it starts to turn golden brown.

I'm not sure anyone can define the moment when the meat-'n-three concept came into being, though it's probably a century or better back in time. What I am sure of is that you find it throughout the South, from Virginia to Louisiana, in various formats.

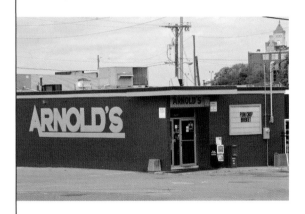

In Tennessee they're on every corner, some in nicer buildings, others in cinderblock shacks or gas stations along the rural routes you drive between Nashville and McMinnville or Sparta. The building is no indication of how good the food is—some of the best food is in some of the most rickety and rundown spaces.

Corporate-culture chains now take the meat-and-three concept to the masses, but things change as they attempt to appeal to everyone—there's no raspberry iced tea or jalapeño popper starter brought to your table at a true meat-and-three. Real ones generally involve a cafeteria-style line: Choose your meat—fried chicken, roast beef with gravy, pork barbecue, chicken livers, catfish, and so on—and pair it with sides. Note I don't say "vegetables," because while you find cucumbers and tomatoes, greens, beans, succotash, and such, there's plenty of starch—mashed potatoes, corn bread, macaroni and cheese, grits—and deep-fried options like cornmeal-crusted okra.

In Nashville, folks like the Arnold family of Arnold's Country Kitchen have turned true meat-'n-three into an art form. Others have modernized the traditional Southern foodways, adapting favorite recipes into fine-dining variations.

You'll find any number of classic meat-'n-three recipes in this book—some in old-school formats, some taken in new directions. There are four takes on mac and cheese, for example, from the adult wonder of Cabana's, made as a grown-up main course with lobster and brie, and Whiskey Kitchen's spicy Southwest-influenced chipotle variation, to Arnold's straightforward meat-'n-three style, perfect for pairing with the catfish recipe they've provided, and Saffire's side for the Chicken Fried Chicken.

Together they underline how the South's foodways evolve to meet the needs of contemporary diners.

THE BANG CANDY COMPANY

1300 CLINTON STREET, SUITE 127, GERMANTOWN/NORTH NASHVILLE
(615) 953-1065
BANGCANDYCOMPANY.COM
CHEF/OWNER: SARAH SOUTHER

I first met Sarah Souther a few years ago, when she was a regular at events at the Nashville Farmers' Market with her Coco-Van, serving hot cocoa and homemade marshmallows of devastating goodness during the cold months. Then, during my days at a city magazine, I had interns Ali and Olivia, who wanted to be food writers. To celebrate the end of the semester, they brought me a box of artisan rosewater-scented, chocolate-dipped marshmallows from the kitchen of Sarah Souther. I was hooked.

Today, Sarah has turned her business into a brick-and-mortar, leaving long lines outside the Bang Candy Company shop at Marathon Motor Works in Germantown, some waiting for a refreshing lunch of soups, salads, and sandwiches, others clamoring for her homemade confections.

I've got a real weakness for her "boozy" salted caramels these days. Even more, her magical simple syrups are now de rigueur on friends' bars, for mixing cocktails. The Sarah special is a glass of Prosecco with one of them added in. I favor the Rosemary Ginger, which has a marvelous ginger beer pop in a little bubbly.

I'm thrilled Sarah's given me a complex confection for the book. "This little delight marries a myriad of tastes and sensations, it is absolutely irresistible," she says. "There are a few steps but don't be put off—it will be worth it in the end!" She's right.

"You will need a mixer, a thermometer, a forcing bag and tip, and a blowtorch amongst the usual kitchen bits and bobs," per Sarah.

MONEY CAN'T BUY HAPPINESS, BUT IT CAN BUY MARSHMALLOWS, WHICH ARE KINDA THE SAME THING.

Brussels Sprouts & Bacon Pizza

(MAKES 4 PERSONAL PIZZAS)

For the dough:

2½ teaspoons active dry yeast
1½ cups warm water
2 cups 00 flour or all-purpose flour
1 cup high-gluten flour or bread flour
2 teaspoons kosher salt

For the toppings:

1 pound bacon, sliced into 16 strips
1 pound Brussels sprouts
1 pound shredded provolone cheese

For the sauce:

3 tablespoons chopped garlic
⅛ teaspoon red pepper flakes
¼ cup bacon fat (or olive oil if preferred)
1 (35-ounce) can crushed tomatoes
    (San Marzano preferred)
1 teaspoon salt
⅓ cup chopped fresh parsley
2 tablespoons chopped fresh basil

To make the dough: Combine yeast and water in a bowl and stir to dissolve. Let sit 5–10 minutes, until yeast blooms and rises to the surface.

Add flours and salt. If using an electric mixer, use the dough hook attachment and mix on low for 4 minutes. Let dough rest 5 minutes, then mix on low for 4 more minutes.

If kneading by hand, lightly flour countertop and knead 200 strokes. Let dough rest 5 minutes, then knead 200 more strokes.

Let dough rise in a loosely covered container (cloth or foil) 1–3 hours, until tripled in size.

Divide into 4 equal portions and lightly flour. For each ball, fold the corners under, forming a smooth skin side on top. Keeping skin side up, continue folding under to create surface tension, until the dough becomes a smooth ball. Cover and let rest in refrigerator overnight.

To prepare the toppings: Cook bacon strips until they just begin to curl but are not yet browned. Chop in ¼-inch strips. Save bacon fat for sauce and Brussels sprouts.

Trim bottoms off Brussels sprouts and cut into quarters. Heat bacon fat on stove top, add sprouts, and cook on medium until soft and just starting to brown.

To make the sauce: Sauté garlic and pepper flakes in bacon fat until garlic is browned. Add tomatoes and salt. Gently simmer for 10 minutes.

Add herbs; gently simmer for 45 minutes more.

Refrigerate overnight or let cool before using.

To make the pizzas: Remove dough from refrigerator and let rest at room temperature 1 hour before using. Put a baking stone on top oven rack and turn on the broiler to heat for 1 hour before baking.

Stretch dough into 10-inch rounds.

Top with sauce first, then provolone, Brussels sprouts, and finally bacon.

Bake directly on stone under the broiler with oven door cracked open (to ensure broiler element stays on). When crust puffs up and back begins to brown, rotate pizza and continue cooking until crust is golden brown all around, 3–5 minutes.

THE NASHVILLE FARMERS' MARKET

If you expect our farmers' market is just a place to buy produce, you're in for a surprise. The powerhouse Nashville Farmers' Market has grown to symbolize the best and most exciting food trends going on in the city. Oh yes, there are a crop of sellers who maintain regular stalls in the market daily, and a larger farm and artisan market, as well as a flea market, on weekends. But there's more to it than that.

Skirting Bicentennial Park in Germantown, just north of the state capitol grounds (and affording a wonderful view of the antebellum capitol building), the Nashville Farmers' Market also has a market house full of some of the most creative restaurants in Nashville, some of which are represented in this book: Arnold Myint's AM@FM, B&C Market Barbecue, Bella Nashville, Chicago Gyro, El Burrito Mexicano, the incredibly popular Jamaicaway, The Original Nooley's Cajun cuisine, Swagruha and many more grace the market house, where half the city comes for lunch.

There's an International Grocery, specializing in South Asian cooking supplies, and during the week a host of artisan bakers and other food purveyors sell their wares from tables in and out of the Market House. A bevy of plant sellers, many selling Tennessee-raised additions for gardens, thrive here, including the permanent Gardens of Babylon.

The market is host to major events, from visits from popular cooking shows like *Top Chef* to chef-driven, hosted dinners featuring culinary experts from Nashville and beyond. Those events also include the Southern Artisan Cheese Festival in 2012 and plenty of food charity–driven occasions.

Cities like New York, San Francisco, Portland, or Seattle may have had such options for a long time, but for us, the Nashville Farmers' Market is a major sign of the progress we've made, especially in the last decade, when it comes to our food community. The market is a bellwether for us, telling us where our food trends are going and reminding us that security in the food community is vital: Indeed, the Nashville Farmers' Market vendors serve some of the city's poorest, as well as its most affluent, every day. Many a restaurant meal begins at the market, and many a home-cooked one as well.

Visit nashvillefarmersmarket.org for more.

BISCUIT LOVE TRUCK

300 4TH AVENUE SOUTH, FRANKLIN, TN 37074
(615) 557-6933
FOR DAILY LOCATION UPDATES, VISIT WWW.FACEBOOK.COM/
BISCUITLOVETRUCK
BISCUITLOVETRUCK.COM
EXECUTIVE CHEF/OWNER: KARL WORLEY

I remember the very first time I tried the Princess biscuit Karl Worley of Biscuit Love has shared for this book. (The name's in homage to hot chicken icon Andre Prince of Prince's Hot Chicken.) I was at the Franklin Farmers' Market, out early, hadn't eaten breakfast, and was starving—and lo and behold, among the many excellent food vendors, I saw Biscuit

Love (then using Jason McConnell's mobile food truck) and headed over. It only took the words "hot chicken" to sell me.

I sat at a picnic table, set my bag of produce next to me, and shot an image of my gorgeous biscuit, with its creamy, textured mustard and fresh pickles to upload to Facebook before I ate. The moment I bit into it, I knew I had something miraculous in my hands. Rich, homemade, grainy mustard and tart pickle hit my taste buds first, then the heat of the chicken, but not enough to make me call for water, like something from Prince's. It was just right, on every level. The use of the flavorful chicken thigh instead of breast meat made the tastes more complex.

Nashville has plenty of takes on our specialty hot chicken, but this is one of my very favorites.

Biscuit Love, part of Nashville's burgeoning food truck movement, has plenty more to love, like the East Nasty, with buttermilk fried chicken, Kenny's farmhouse cheddar, and sausage gravy, and the Gertie, with homemade banana jam, peanut butter with pretzel crunch (they make it themselves), and Olive & Sinclair chocolate gravy. Oh, and grab a side of cheese grits while you're at it. Try it, feel the biscuit love.

THE PRINCESS BISCUIT

(SERVES 10)

For the chicken brine:

2 cups buttermilk

2 tablespoons kosher salt

2 tablespoons freshly ground black pepper

2 teaspoons granulated garlic

2 teaspoons granulated onion

2 tablespoons smoked paprika

10 boneless, skinless chicken thighs

For the biscuits:

1½ teaspoons rapid-rise dry yeast

¼ cup warm water (around 115°F)

4 teaspoons sugar, divided

2 cups soft winter wheat flour

2 teaspoons baking powder

½ teaspoon baking soda

1 teaspoon salt

⅓ cup butter plus ¼ to ⅓ cup butter, melted

1 cup full-fat buttermilk

For the fried chicken and dip:

Enough peanut oil for frying
    (1 cup reserved after frying for dip)

1 cup all-purpose flour

1 large egg

1 teaspoon baking powder

1 teaspoon smoked paprika

1 teaspoon salt

1 teaspoon pepper

1 teaspoon granulated garlic

1 teaspoon granulated onion

1½ cups water

10 tablespoons cayenne pepper

For assembly:

Honey

Creole mustard

Dill pickles slices

To brine the chicken: Mix all the ingredients except the chicken in a bowl. Add chicken and allow to brine overnight.

To make the biscuits: Mix yeast, water, and 2 teaspoons sugar in a large bowl and allow yeast to bloom for 30 minutes.

Whisk together flour, baking powder, baking soda, salt, and remaining 2 teaspoons of sugar. Add ⅓ cup butter, buttermilk, and yeast mixture to dry ingredients and stir with hands to just combine, being careful not to overwork the dough. Cover dough and let rest in a warm area for 30 minutes to rise.

Place dough on a floured surface and roll it out to ¾ inch thick. Cut biscuits with biscuit cutter. Nestle together on a buttered sheet pan and brush tops with butter. Allow to rest and rise for 15 minutes. Meanwhile, preheat oven to 425°F.

Bake for 12 minutes, or until tops are golden brown. Remove from oven and brush immediately with butter.

To prepare the fried chicken and dip: Add peanut oil to frying pan and place over heat. Using a deep-fry thermometer, heat the oil to 350°F.

Whisk all the ingredients except the cayenne pepper together.

Remove the chicken from the brine and dry with paper towels. Dip the chicken thighs into batter mixture and place chicken into hot oil, being careful not to overcrowd.

Fry for 7–8 minutes or until the internal temperature of the chicken reaches 165°F.

Remove 1 cup of oil from the oil used for frying the chicken, being careful not to spill, as it is very hot. Mix with cayenne pepper in a heatproof bowl. Dip chicken into mixture, and allow it to rest on a wire rack for 1 minute.

To assemble: Slice biscuits in half. Place chicken onto biscuit and top with honey, Creole mustard, and 3 dill pickle slices.

BLVD Nashville

2013 Belmont Boulevard, Belmont/Vanderbilt
(615) 385-2422
BLVDNASHVILLE.COM
Chef/Owner: Arnold Myint

Arnold Myint is the wunderkind of the Nashville food scene grown up. The Nashville native grew up dividing his time between here and South Asia, where his family originated. He made a first career as a competitive, then professional ice skater. Being from a family with a gift for food (his mother, Patti, owns and operates the wonderful International Market & Restaurant nearby), he's now parlayed his culinary talents not only into several of the city's best and most innovative eateries, but also into a place on *Top Chef* Season 7 and a host of other media appearances—with more coming.

In 2013 he closed his incredibly popular concept restaurant Cha-Cha and replaced it with BLVD, a bistro-style restaurant with a delightful menu of creative sandwiches, marvelous entrees (the Salmon n' Grits particularly), and an inventive chef's tasting menu. There's also a marvelous Sunday brunch, featuring the likes of a Local Feta Omelet, Maple Waffle, Quinoa Cassoulet, and an excellent Croque Madame.

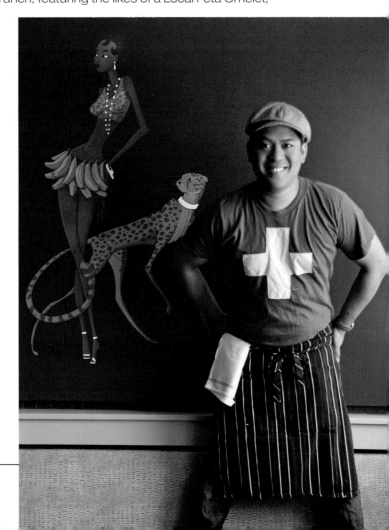

Myint is also responsible for one of the best additions to the downtown farmers' market—his AM@FM is fresh fine dining that has the lunch crowd downtown returning almost daily, with huge, verdant salads, marvelous sandwiches and wraps to go, and a glass of wine if you have time to linger. His other locales, Suzy Wong's House of Yum downtown and PM, also in Belmont, are the kind of boutique gems you find yourself drawn to again and again, because Myint excels at that atmosphere.

I've long been a fan of Arnold's culinary skills, but you can't help appreciating his broad wit, his showmanship, and his dramatic talents as well. There's no one else quite like him in Nashville.

These Brussels sprouts are a perfect spicy side dish for a host of meals.

BRUSSELS SPROUTS

(YIELD DETERMINED BY COOK)

Chef Myint says, "This is a recipe that isn't standardized. I believe that the beauty of cooking is finding a balance based on your personal palate. Just remember, Thai chili peppers are spicy!"

Diced butter cubes
Roughly crushed Spanish Marcona almonds
Chopped Thai chili peppers
Thinly sliced red onion
White balsamic vinegar
Brussels sprout petals*
AM Smoked Salt (available at arnoldmyint.com/shop)
Shaved Pecorino Romano

In a sauté pan, heat butter, almonds, Thai chili, and red onion. Allow butter to slightly brown and other components to sweat and slightly caramelize.

Deglaze the pan with vinegar and add the Brussels sprout petals. Toss the petals and sprinkle AM Smoked Salt as desired.

Remove from heat and finish with shaved Pecorino Romano.

*Note: In preparing your Brussels sprouts, pick the outer petals until you hit the center core. Sadly, in this process we do not use the center.

Burger Up

2901 12th Avenue South, 12South
(615) 279-3767
burger-up.com

401b Cool Springs Boulevard, Franklin
(615) 503-9892

Executive Chef/Owner: Miranda Whitcomb Pontes

We got to know Miranda Whitcomb Pontes first with the coffee-centric restaurant Frothy Monkey in the 12South neighborhood before moving on to Burger Up, a burger concept restaurant that relies on sustainable, organic meats. When she created the concept, the movie *Food, Inc.* was freshly out and on everyone's minds, and she wanted an alternative to the factory farmed foods The first thing on her agenda was to source the very best possible meats, and she did that via Williamson County's Triple L Ranch. She followed that up by sourcing other necessary products at a growing number of local farms in the Middle Tennessee area.

One of the fabulous things about Burger Up, of course, is the fact that not all the burgers are actually beef. They do a killer Citrus Salmon burger, for example, and a really great lamb burger. I must admit, I favor the old-school Woodstock, with Jack Daniel's maple ketchup.

But the pimento cheese–topped Ramsey Burger is a must-try. Pimento cheese is another longtime Southern favorite, and there's a wonderful story that makes it even better. Miranda first used the recipe for the "Mrs. Ida" on the menu at Frothy Monkey, then moved on to reimagine it as the Ramsey Burger at Burger Up.

"A dear friend's mother, Mrs. Ida Ramsey, from Viola, Tennessee, had a special pimento cheese recipe she kindly shared with me," says Miranda. "Mrs. Ida made all her recipes with love, wrote and published a number of cookbooks, and had a passion for feeding folks."

The Ramsey Burger

Assemble per person:

5.5-ounce burger patty, grilled medium
    (Burger Up uses Triple L Ranch beef* 80/20.)
2 ounces Miss Ida's Pimento Cheese (recipe at right)
Thinly sliced red onion
Bibb or butter lettuce
3–4 of your favorite pickle chips (The thicker
    the better.)
Toasted bun

*Note: You may order Triple L Ranch beef at lllranch.com.

Miss Ida's Pimento Cheese

(YIELD: ENOUGH FOR AT LEAST 8 BURGERS)

1 pound grated (largest grate) yellow cheddar
    (Burger Up uses Sweetwater Valley.**)
⅔ cup mayonnaise (Duke's preferred)
2 tablespoons sour cream
3 tablespoons pickle juice (your favorite)
1 tablespoon hot sauce (your favorite)
¼ white onion, grated
Pinch of kosher salt
1 red bell pepper, grilled, peeled, and diced

Add all the ingredients to a bowl and mix with a wooden spoon or rubber spatula. Adjust seasoning (salt, pickle juice, or hot sauce) to your taste

**Note: Find Sweetwater Valley cheeses at sweetwatervalley.com.

CABANA RESTAURANT

1910 BELCOURT AVENUE, HILLSBORO VILLAGE
(615) 577-2262
CABANANASHVILLE.COM
EXECUTIVE CHEF: BRIAN UHL
OWNERS: RANDY RAYBURN, CRAIG CLIFT, AND BRIAN UHL

Cabana, one of the extraordinary restaurants under the auspices of Randy Rayburn, Craig Clift, and Brian Uhl, is a place you go for pure enjoyment. Set in Hillsboro Village within walking distance of Sunset Grill and plenty of other very good restaurants, you choose Cabana because of the atmosphere—and the marvelous menu, which is Southern comfort food made sleek and intriguing, given the creative talents of Uhl, whose expertise can't be understated.

The real fun is that much of the restaurant is divided into large, semiprivate booths, lushly cushioned and curtained, so that your party can enjoy a bit of private conversation and personal space. The concept works well, whether your goal is to have a business dinner or celebrate a little time with friends. You can bring a loaded iPod to dock or even watch the big game within your cabana while you sip on wine (it's an exceptional wine list, given the presence of Craig Clift).

Start out with the lump crab hush puppies or the coffee-and-cocoa-crusted venison carpaccio (always trust Uhl with game meats). When you get to dinner, the Tennessee rainbow trout or perhaps the peach BBQ pork shanks definitely appeal. Finish up with the daily cheesecake or cobbler selection.

Cabana thrives by being experiential—and you'll never regret a moment of it.

CRAB CAKES WITH ASIAN SLAW & MANGO CHILI SAUCE

(SERVES 4)

For the Asian slaw:

1 head Napa cabbage, sliced ½ inch thick

2 tablespoons sesame oil

1 cup sour cream

3 tablespoons sweet chili sauce

2 teaspoons rice wine vinegar

Salt and pepper to taste

For the crab cakes:

1 pound lump crab

1 red bell pepper, diced small

2 tablespoons sliced chives

1 lemon, juiced

1 teaspoon Dijon, or to taste

2–3 ounces mayonnaise

Salt and pepper to taste

3–4 tablespoons ground panko bread crumbs

For the mango chili sauce:

1 cup mango puree

3 tablespoons sweet chili

1 teaspoon sambal chili or other hot chili sauce, to taste

For the Asian slaw, mix all the ingredients in a mixing bowl and refrigerate for at least an hour.

Fold together all the ingredients for the crab cakes and form them into 3- to 4-ounce patties. Sauté in a nonstick pan with a little oil until golden brown on both sides.

Mix the mango puree, sweet chili sauce, and sambal together for the sauce.

Plate crab cakes on the slaw, and drizzle with sauce before serving.

LOBSTER & BRIE "MAC AND CHEESE" WITH BENTON'S SMOKY MOUNTAIN COUNTRY HAM CRISP

(SERVES 4)

While there are several traditional takes on the Southern standard macaroni and cheese in this book, this particular variation is quite unlike anything else—it makes use of rich, creamy brie, heavy cream, and Parmesan, paired with lobster meat for something deliciously decadent yet still in the realm of "comfort food." This is definitely the most grown-up method provided here for mac and cheese, and note they gave it to me with playful quotes around "mac and cheese"—this ain't your five-year-old's take on the dish, and that's as it should be. You can find Benton's Country Ham at bentonscountryhams2.com.

2 cups heavy cream

4 cups cooked ditalini pasta (or any small-cut macaroni)

Salt and black pepper to taste

5 ounces brie, cut into small cubes

1 ounce Parmesan cheese, freshly grated

8 ounces cooked lobster meat

8–10 slices Benton's Country Ham prosciutto (or your favorite prosciutto), sliced paper thin

1 teaspoon olive oil

2 tablespoons chopped chives, for garnish

In a large sauté pan, bring heavy cream to a boil. Add the cooked pasta and reduce cream by one-third. Season with salt and pepper. Stir in the cheeses and let it thicken, then add the lobster meat. Heat until the lobster is warmed through and the cheese is completely melted.

Brush the ham slices with olive oil and bake on a sheet pan for 6–8 minutes in a 350°F oven (or cook until the ham is crisp).

Spoon the "mac and cheese" onto a plate. Top with crispy country ham, sprinkle with chives, and garnish with a lobster claw.

Caffe Nonna

4427 Murphy Road, Sylvan Park
(615) 463-0133
CAFFENONNA.COM
Executive Chef/Owner: Dan Maggipinto

Caffe Nonna, a magical little neighborhood Italian restaurant located in Sylvan Park, is the epitome of comfort food. A little off busier West End, the area boasts wonderful vintage homes and cottages appealing to young families. Within the walls of Caffe Nonna, locals and nonlocals alike converge to consume incredible pasta dishes and wood-fired pizzas.

Start out your order with the Tuscan Bruschetta or Mussels Apulia, then move on perhaps to a Nonna Salad with fried calamari added or a larger meal—the Seafood Angelini is popular, and so is the Nonna Lasagna. Or you can go for a pizza, from a basic Margherita to the limits of your imagination with a plethora of delicious add-ons. There's quite a respectable wine list, too.

When ordering pasta, you can choose your pasta type, sauce, and additions as well. Better yet, take a jar of the marvelously spicy arrabiata (I always order this one) or regular marinara home with you. In doing so, you support the Zoe Marie Foundation, a

Partner in Hope with St. Jude's Children's Hospital. Named for Chef Dan's lovely daughter in memory of her tragic struggle with brain cancer, the Zoe Marie Foundation marries fantastic foods with the best of causes. (You can order these sauces and other products from Chef Dan and Caffe Nonna wherever you are, via nonnasgourmetfoods.com.)

SMOKED SALMON WITH ORECCHIETTE PASTA

(SERVES 4–6)

1 pound orecchiette pasta

¼ small red onion, sliced thin

3 plum tomatoes, seeded and diced

2 tablespoons chopped garlic

½ cup capers

Olive oil for sautéing

8 ounces smoked salmon, rolled and
   sliced into strips

¼ cup grainy mustard

1 cup white wine

¾ cup mascarpone

¼ cup chopped dill

4 cups baby arugula

Kosher salt

Cracked black pepper

¼ cup basil, cut into thin strips,
   for garnish

Fill up a pot with enough cold water to cook the pasta. Add some salt to it and let it come to a boil. Cook pasta per package instructions once you get the sauce going. Then strain and toss in a little bit of olive oil so it doesn't stick.

In a large sauté pan on medium-high heat, add the onion, tomato, garlic, capers, and olive oil. Sauté for 3–4 minutes, stirring to blend. Scrape the bottom to release the bits of flavor to create the foundation of the sauce.

Add the smoked salmon and grainy mustard. Sauté another 1–2 minutes. Pour in the white wine and reduce by one-fourth. Add the mascarpone and stir to combine. Reduce for 2–3 minutes, longer if needed, to slightly thicken.

Add the pasta, dill, and arugula. Heat through and toss to combine. Taste and season with salt and pepper. You can add a bit more wine to thin out and stretch the sauce if necessary. The sauce should cling to the pasta.

Portion the pasta onto plates and garnish with the basil, and cheese if you like.

One sign of growth in the local food community is indubitably the proliferation of artisan foods in Middle Tennessee. Kathleen Cotter's Bloomy Rind artisan cheese shop is proof positive of that, along with local organic Porter Road Butcher, which shares premises with the Bloomy Rind in East Nashville. Cotter started out in human resources, but a few years ago decided she was ready to shift gears and contemplated where her passions lay.

"It came down to cheese and chocolate," she says. At that time, Scott Witherow of Olive & Sinclair was making waves in the chocolate world, so Cotter went for cheese. After a sabbatical spent learning about the American artisan cheese movement, including cheese boot camp at Murray's in New York City, she set herself up as a cheesemonger. She hawked fine cheeses privately, including fine representations of Southern cheesemaking, at the Nashville Farmers' Market.

Cotter focused on representative Southern products like Green Hill from Georgia's Sweet Grass Dairy and a few others that really struck her, some outside our region (the South traditionally hasn't had an artisan cheese culture). "Ascutney Mountain [Cobb Hill Cheese, Vermont], a magical alpine-style cheese, was an early favorite of mine," she says. "And Barely Buzzed [Beehive Cheese Co., Utah] is such a strange, delicious concept with a coffee and lavender rub on the rind. Then came Wisconsin's Dunbarton Blue (Roelli Cheese), a natural rind cheddar with bits of blue in it, which led to more, and more." As her interest grew, business thrived.

With her shop open and past the two-year mark on her annual Southern Artisan Cheese Festival, Kathleen Cotter's really showing local residents and restaurants how to do cheese just right. Come in, try, buy, and go home happy.

The Bloomy Rind, 501 Gallatin Avenue, (615) 429-9648, bloomyrind.com.

Capitol Grille

231 6th Avenue North (Hermitage Hotel), Downtown
(615) 345-7116
CAPITOLGRILLENASHVILLE.COM
Executive Chef: Tyler Brown

If anyone can be credited with changing the farm-to-fork ethos in Nashville, it has to be Tyler Brown. I'd be lying if I said he wasn't one of my personal heroes for the paradigm shift he and the folks at Capitol Grille and the Hermitage Hotel have brought about in terms of showing the public what sustainability and land preservation are all about. Tyler and the whole crew at Capitol Grille have spent the past several years developing a vast garden at the Land Trust for Tennessee's farm at Glen Leven. Here, they've worked tirelessly to raise a huge percentage of the produce used at the Capitol Grille, inspiring others to follow suit as they go.

Recently the hotel invested in a 245-acre property, Double H Farms, to build on their sustainability commitment. Here they'll continue to raise cattle, honey, and a variety of crops destined for a place at your table at the Capitol Grille.

Tyler himself is the kind of affable guy whose company you can't help but enjoy, especially if you understand the depth of what he's doing. His awareness of the food as part of the land translates, with the aid of his Johnson and Wales training, into an understanding of cookery that means every meal at the Capitol Grille is something special.

My husband and I have enjoyed many a dinner at the Capitol Grille—it's the kind of place where you can look around and see celebrities, tourists, politicians, and mostly regular people, all of whom are there to appreciate the fine food. The bar is set high on everything, and whether you just want old-fashioned fried chicken or something more elaborate, you'll be pleased with the result.

Hanger Steak with Vegetable Frites
& Double-Fried French Fries

(SERVES 8)

Chimichurri

⅓ cup extra-virgin olive oil

1 clove garlic, peeled and finely chopped or pressed

1 cup well-rinsed parsley leaves, lightly packed

1 cup well-rinsed cilantro leaves, lightly packed

1 teaspoon salt

¼ teaspoon freshly ground black pepper

1 tablespoon sherry vinegar

¼ cup minced red onion (or add chunks to food processor before herbs)

1 tablespoon capers, rinsed

In a small food processor, combine the olive oil and garlic and run until the garlic is well distributed. (If you don't feel like mincing the onion by hand, you can add it in chunks now, but it won't look as nice.) If you don't have a small food processor, you might need to make a double batch, as a full-size machine probably won't work well on this small quantity.

Add the parsley, cilantro, salt, pepper, and vinegar and process until minced but with still a bit of texture left in the leaves.

Remove from the food processor and mix in the onions and capers.

Let rest at least 30 minutes, then taste and adjust salt, pepper, and vinegar as needed.

Hanger Steak

4 pounds trimmed hanger steak

⅓ cup chimichurri (recipe to left)

Marinate the hanger steak overnight with ⅓ cup of chimichurri (reserve remainder for later use).

Vegetable Frites

1 fennel bulb, cut into 8 wedges

16 baby carrots, peeled or cleaned with a wet towel

16 pearl onions

1 large celery root, peeled and cut into batonettes

1 cup water

1 cup rice wine vinegar

1 cup sugar

2 bay leaves

3 sprigs thyme

½ teaspoon salt

Preheat oven to 350°F.

Combine all the ingredients in a Dutch oven with the lid, bring to a boil on stovetop, and braise in the oven for 1 hour.

Remove from oven and allow vegetables to cool in the liquid.

Remove the vegetables from the liquid and reserve liquid for another use. Pat the veggies dry, then lay them on a baking sheet that has been drizzled with olive oil.

Bake at 350°F, until crispy. Reseason with salt, pepper, and herbs if you like.

DOUBLE-FRIED FRENCH FRIES

1 pound Kennebec potatoes
1 pound sweet potatoes
2 quarts canola oil
1 tablespoon fine-grain sea salt
1 teaspoon freshly ground black pepper

Peel potatoes on the sides, leaving the ends with the skin on. Cut the potatoes into ⅓-inch slices and then slice into ⅓-inch sticks.

Fill a large bowl with water and soak potatoes, submerged, for at least 30 minutes and up to 24 hours. This will help remove the excess starch from the potatoes and keep them from oxidizing.

Heat oil in a heavy stockpot fitted with a deep-fry thermometer to 325°F.

Remove potatoes from the water, and pat dry to remove excess water. Add 2 handfuls of potatoes to hot oil. There should be at least 1 inch of oil above the potatoes. Par-cook until potatoes are light brown, 5–7 minutes. Remove potatoes, gently shaking off excess oil, and let drain on rack. Repeat until all of the potatoes are par-cooked.

Raise heat of oil to 350°F.

Cook potatoes again, 2 handfuls at a time, until golden brown, about 2 minutes. Remove from oil, shake off excess oil, and season lightly in a bowl with salt and pepper. Repeat until all potatoes are cooked.

Plating the dish: Grill the hanger steak to preferred doneness. Crisp up the Vegetables Frites by sautéing lightly in olive oil. French fries should ideally be made right before serving. Arrange on the plate and garnish the steak with the remaining chimichurri.

Spring Trout

(SERVES 8–10)

Tennessee is landlocked, and much ado is made about getting fresh fish in Nashville. These days it's reasonable to expect that our fine-dining establishments have had their seafood flown in directly from the coasts, and that it will be fresh. However, we also have the advantage of plenty of lakes and rivers; because of that, freshwater fish abound, and the possibilities for cooking them are endless. This particular trout recipe will be appreciatively received by anyone who's a trout fan. If you wish to use the Capitol Grille trout source, you can order from Sunburst Trout Farms in North Carolina via sunbursttrout.com/products.

2 cups hominy

1 tablespoon salt

1 teaspoon black pepper

½ cup dry-roasted peanuts

8–10 trout fillets (Capitol Grille uses Sunburst Trout Farms trout.)

4 ounces peanut oil

Lightly roast the hominy on a cookie sheet in a 400°F oven for about 30 minutes, stirring twice. Place the roasted hominy, salt, pepper, and peanuts in a food mill (KitchenAid preferred) and dial the setting to coarse grind. Dredge the trout in the seasoned hominy mixture, then shallow-fry the fish to golden brown in peanut oil.

SALAD WITH GREEN GODDESS DRESSING

(MAKES ABOUT 2 PINTS DRESSING)

A flavorful side dish with any meal, especially beef or fish.

5 cloves garlic

1 shallot

1 tablespoon goat cheese

3 tablespoons Dijon mustard

2 ounces white wine vinegar

Juice of 1 lemon

5 egg yolks

4 anchovies

2 tablespoons chopped fresh parsley

1 tablespoon chopped fresh tarragon

1 cup blended oil

Salad greens

Combine garlic, shallot, goat cheese, Dijon, white wine vinegar, lemon juice, and yolks in a blender. Once smooth, add the herbs and emulsify the oil into it.

Drizzle dressing directly on salad greens.

SAUTÉED SWISS CHARD

(SERVES 8)

Greens tend to be available for a large portion of the year in Tennessee, and often we're at a loss for how to serve them creatively. This method for Swiss chard really emphasizes the full flavor of both leaves and stems and will have you wanting seconds of your vegetables.

2 pounds Swiss chard

4 teaspoons butter, divided

⅛ teaspoon pepper

½ teaspoon salt

1 tablespoon vinegar or lemon juice

Rinse chard and separate the stems from leaves. Cut stems into 2-inch pieces; cut leaves crosswise into 1-inch strips.

In a saucepan, add 2 teaspoons butter. Add chard stems to pan and sauté about 5 minutes. Add leaves and cook another 5 minutes. Add remaining 2 teaspoons butter and pepper.

Mound the chard in the center of a serving plate and drizzle with vinegar or lemon juice.

BLUEBERRY COBBLER COCKTAIL

The Oak Bar at the Hermitage Hotel is known for its astonishingly wonderful cocktails. A couple years ago, Tyler Brown set a precedent by arranging for single-barrel whiskey direct from the Jack Daniel's distillery in Lynchburg, Tennessee, and the resultant cocktails were amazing. There's nothing that comes out of the Oak Bar that doesn't dazzle. In this case, they've sent over a cocktail that will appeal not only in spring, but in all seasons, in spite of its spring-like name. Of course, fresh local blueberries will always make this the best possible beverage, and when I told them I wanted a locally based cocktail, they went straight to the berries.

2 ounces Hangar One Straight Vodka

1 tablespoon opal basil leaves

½ ounce simple syrup

¾ ounce St. Germain elderflower liqueur

Juice of 1 lemon wedge

2–3 ice cubes

1 tablespoon blueberries

½–1 ounce soda

Shake together all ingredients except blueberries and soda with ice cubes to chill.

Pour soda and place blueberries in a martini or rocks glass. Strain cocktail ingredients into the glass over berries and serve.

DELVIN FARMS

The farm-to-fork movement isn't brand-new in Nashville: Some of our farmers, like the Delvin family, have been preaching the gospel of sustainability and responsible agriculture for a long time now. With one of the area's oldest and largest CSAs, Delvin represents some of the best of our farming community.

In the early 1970s Hank Delvin (pictured right) worked his way through college selling fresh farm produce. He had a job in the futures market, buying and selling grain, but his work led him back to the farm. He used his agri-culture degree and started conventionally, but as wife Cindy tells it, once they had children, they grew concerned about the chemicals and moved back to doing things the way his father and grandfather had. No one called it organic or sustainable then, but that's what it was. From 1972 onward, they sold their produce through grocery stores and to restaurants like Shoney's.

Pursued by friends and neighbors wanting to buy produce directly, the Delvins came upon the CSA concept in the late '90s, when son Eric sent them to a conference at Jekyll Island, Georgia. They researched the concept and determined it was a "way to satisfy the hunger people have to come to the farm and be part of it, without us setting up a farm stand." They had an easy time being certified organic.

Planning began in January, and their first shares arrived May 1—pretty, neat boxes of lush vegetables. Son Hank Jr. (pictured left) and daughter Amy returned to Tennessee with their families to work with them, and a decade later Delvin is a mainstay for families, farmers' markets, and restaurants, including Saffire, Sloco, City House, Rolf & Daughters, Yellow Porch, and Burger Up.

The huge farm produces astonishing varieties of fruits and vegetables, honey, and more; offers farm tours for schoolchildren; and underlines what it means to be a true family farm in the era of big corporate operations.

"Know your farmer if you want to know about your food," Hank Delvin tells me at the Franklin Farmers' Market. "Just like you know your banker, your doctor, or your lawyer." Sound advice.

CITY HOUSE

1222 4TH AVENUE NORTH, GERMANTOWN
(615) 736-5838
CITYHOUSENASHVILLE.COM
EXECUTIVE CHEF/OWNER: TANDY WILSON

City House is one of my favorite places in town, and I simply don't get there often enough since it's in Germantown, well north of my Franklin home. That's a pity, because Tandy Wilson serves up some of the best, most innovative food in Nashville. He tends to eschew personal publicity, but that hasn't kept him and City House from national note, everywhere from fashion and culture magazines to nominations for James Beard Awards, simply because of his talent and his creativity in the kitchen.

I first met Tandy at a party in Patrick Martin's home kitchen, as he strode through with a plate full of strips of meat, fresh from the grill, proffering it to fellow guests. I tried it, so did my husband—it was delicious. "What is it?" I asked.

"Pig's heart," replied Tandy, without a trace of a smile. From that moment he joined the small list of people (Tyler Brown, Jason McConnell, and himself) that have taught me to eat what they give me without even asking what it is on the plate.

At City House you'll find everything on the menu from oxtail stew to octopus pasta

to rather more simple dishes like the pork meatballs, and I recommend all of it. They also easily have one of the best bars in Nashville, the kind of bar where you don't mind going in alone, sitting on a stool, and ordering wine, cocktails, and dinner alone—someone you know will show up eventually, and if they don't, you won't care.

Every cocktail is extraordinary (the wine list is also very good), and among them this offering stands out. Made with Corsair gin, which is a true juniper and citrus lover's gin, with a hint of grapefruit note, it's guaranteed to make you happy on a warm summer night.

PORCH POUNDER

1½ ounces Corsair Artisan Gin*
1½ ounces Martini and Rossi Roscato Vermouth
1 ounce lemon juice
¼ ounce Lazzaroni Amaretto
2 dashes Fee Bros. Rhubarb Bitters**
Splash of soda

Build this drink in a pint jar, top it with soda, gently rotate the glass in your hand to lightly mix together the components, and serve with a lemon wheel to garnish.

*Note: You can find Corsair gin and products from the Corsair Artisan microdistillery in most major cities; find out more at corsairartisan.com.

**Note: Do not substitute! Omit if you don't have Fee Bros. Rhubarb Bitters. They can be found at many online gourmet sources and Amazon.com.

THE COCOA TREE

THECOCOATREE.COM
CHEF/OWNER: BETHANY THOUIN

I first met Bethany when she had a lovely, tiny shop in Franklin about six years ago, where she was redefining what artisan chocolate was for the residents of Williamson County, who were used to the stuff they bought at chain markets. Shortly thereafter she moved the Cocoa Tree to Germantown on the north side of the city, and her fans continued to grow.

I stopped by regularly for chocolate espresso beans and a chance to check out whatever she was doing new. As of press time she may be moving on to a new location, but for those wanting her coveted chocolates outside Nashville, ordering online is readily available.

Thouin's gotten plenty of media attention for her exquisite handmade truffles, including those inspired by music artists who work in Nashville. She's worked with CMT Television, creating signature truffles paying tribute to the honorees for CMT Artist of the Year Awards. She created sweet treats using the inspiration of everyone from Carrie Underwood to the Zac Brown Band. Each one possesses elements that reflect the personality and work of the artist.

When asked to participate in this project, Bethany thoughtfully provided recipes for truffles inspired by two of the city's favorites, Oprah Winfrey and Amy Grant.

AMY'S BALSAMIC RASPBERRY TRUFFLES

(MAKES 28 17-GRAM TRUFFLES)

"The one that knows the bitter and the sweet."
INSPIRED BY AMY GRANT

8 ounces dark chocolate (72% cocoa content)
½ cup heavy cream
2 tablespoons raspberry puree
2 tablespoons balsamic vinegar
1 pound dark chocolate (for dipping)
¼ cup dried raspberries (for topping)

See "To Make the Truffles" on the next page.

SOFIA'S SWEET POTATO TRUFFLES

(MAKES 34 17-GRAM TRUFFLES)

"The one that's good for the soul."
INSPIRED BY OPRAH WINFREY.

8 ounces milk chocolate (41% cocoa content)
¼ cup heavy cream
¼ cup sweet potato puree (recipe below)
1 pound milk chocolate (for dipping)
1 ounce dried sweet potato curls (for topping)

Sweet Potato Puree

¼ cup heavy cream
½ cup baked sweet potato
¼ teaspoon nutmeg
¼ teaspoon cinnamon

In a saucepan, bring cream just to a boil.

Spoon baked sweet potato into a blender. Add cream, nutmeg, and cinnamon and blend until smooth.

TO MAKE THE TRUFFLES

Ganache: Bring 2 cups of water just to a boil in a 2½-quart saucepan. Place chocolate inside a glass or stainless bowl that fits just inside the saucepan. Melt the chocolate over the steam until it reaches 100°F. Remove the bowl from the steam.

Bring the heavy cream just to a boil and pour it immediately into the melted chocolate, stirring vigorously until the mixture is silky smooth.

At this time add your other ingredients to create exciting flavors. Amy uses purees, spices, liqueurs, and so on to bring her truffles to life: balsamic vinegar and raspberries or sweet potato puree in the case of these two truffles.

Refrigerate the ganache until it has the consistency of pudding. This should take at least 20 minutes. Then beat the ganache with a hand mixer for 15 seconds. Let the ganache rest until it reaches room temperature.

The ganache should now be ready for making truffle centers. Scoop the ganache onto parchment paper using a small ice-cream scoop. With the palms of your hands, gently roll the scooped ganache into perfectly round balls. If the ganache is too soft to roll, refrigerate for several minutes.

Dipping and topping: Now you are ready to dip the truffles. Generously cover the palms of both of your hands with tempered chocolate. (See tempering instructions at right.) Pick up a ganache center and roll it in the palms of your hands until it is thoroughly coated. Set on parchment paper; continue until all centers have been coated. When the first coat is hardened, coat your palms with tempered chocolate again and cover truffles with a second coat.

Finish the truffle by sprinkling dried raspberries or placing a small sweet potato curl on the top before the chocolate sets up. The wet chocolate will act as glue, keeping your toppings in place.

Store your truffles at room temperature. They should be enjoyed within 5 days.

How to Temper Chocolate

When you melt chocolate, you take it from its tempered state to its untempered state. So, in order to get the beautiful appearance back, you have to temper it, or "make it behave."

You will need:

1 pound chocolate, chopped into bite-size pieces
1 microwave-safe bowl
1 rubber spatula
1 digital thermometer

Place ⅔ pound of the chocolate in a microwave-safe bowl. Melt the chocolate, stirring at 30-second intervals until the chocolate reaches 115°F (110°F if it is white chocolate). Add a small handful of the remaining ⅓ pound of chocolate bits to the melted chocolate and stir constantly. Repeat this step until all the chocolate has been stirred in and melted or until the chocolate has reached 89°F.

At this point the chocolate should be tempered. You can test it by dipping the end of a plastic utensil into the chocolate and letting it rest for 2 minutes. The chocolate should set up quickly with a shiny finish. When you are tempering chocolate, the temperature of the kitchen should be cool, ideally around 68°F.

CORK & COW

403 MAIN STREET, FRANKLIN
(615) 538-6021
CORKANDCOW.COM
EXECUTIVE CHEF/OWNER: JASON MCCONNELL
CHEF: CARL SCHULTHEIS

Once upon a time, the building at 403 Main Street in Franklin was Jason McConnell's authentic Mexican venture, SOL. This worked very well, but the bellwethers of the local restaurant scene changed, and soon the front bar of SOL and front room permanently morphed into 55South, and so it remains today. Very recently, Jason opted to turn Sol into a new format, Franklin's first true local steak house. Having been there for the soft opening, I can tell you it was a success from go.

Cork & Cow, with its cork walls and vintage cleavers, clean white tablecloths, and close-set tables, gives you European intimacy with a wholly American attitude. Begin your meal by ordering a cocktail, then the beef carpaccio or warm marinated olives to start. For my money, the New York strip and the rib eye are the way to go, medium rare, because this is truly good beef. Add the triple threat of béarnaise, lump crab, and roasted red peppers, and if you've got an appetite going, perhaps a grilled lobster tail. There are multiple takes on the potato, try the salt-crusted baked potato or the fries with malt vinegar aioli. Order the bacon-wrapped Brussels sprouts on the side (these are marvelous).

Of course, Cork & Cow pairs other sides with their steaks, including pastas, and this one is utterly delicious.

BUTTERNUT ROTOLO

(SERVES 6–8 AS AN APPETIZER OR SIDE DISH)

This is a recipe for an Italian rolled pasta. It takes some time to prep, but it's a great do-ahead dish that will impress.

For the filling:

½ butternut squash
Salt and pepper to taste
1 cup goat cheese
1 cup ricotta cheese
1 tablespoon fresh thyme, finely chopped
Pinch of nutmeg
2 cups sautéed spinach

For the pasta:

4 cups flour
6 eggs

For cooking:

1 tablespoon olive oil

For the quick sauce:

2 tablespoons crushed hazelnuts
1 teaspoon fresh thyme, finely chopped
Splash of white wine for deglazing
2 or 3 pats cold butter

To make the filling: Preheat oven to 350°F.

Cut the squash in half; reserve one half for another use. Remove the seeds from the remaining half. Season with salt, pepper, and olive oil. Bake covered for 45 minutes.

Mix all the ingredients except the spinach gently by hand.

To make the pasta: Place flour on a cutting board or in a bowl. Make a well in the center and place eggs in the middle. Whisk eggs with a fork, then with floured hands mix together until incorporated and silky smooth. Cover or wrap with plastic and allow to rest for 30 minutes.

Assembling the rotolo: You should be thinking *jelly roll of pasta,* so the directions are for spreading, rolling, wrapping with cheesecloth, poaching, and sautéing.

Roll out the pasta with a pasta machine into sheets that are the full width of your machine and approximately 8 inches in length. Spread a layer of the squash mixture, then spread some of the spinach over the top of each sheet of pasta.

Roll each sheet to form a "jelly roll" of filled pasta. Wrap with cheesecloth and tie with butcher's twine on each end.

Bring water to a simmer in a pot that you can fit your wrapped pasta rolls into. Poach the rolls for 10–12 minutes to cook the dough

Remove and chill.

Cooking the rotolo: Remove cheesecloth once the rolls have chilled and cut each roll into pieces that are 2 inches wide. Heat 1 tablespoon olive oil in a sauté pan and sear the rotolo on each side until golden brown, then remove.

Making a quick pan sauce: Once you take the rotolo out of the pan, you can throw in some crushed hazelnuts and chopped thyme, then deglaze with white wine and finish with a few pieces of cold butter. Season with salt and pepper, then pour over the top of rotolo.

CORK & COW COCKTAILS

One of the things Jason McConnell has always excelled at is making sure the cocktail culture of his restaurants defies the ordinary. Both Red Pony and Cork & Cow have intimate bars that you can make into your entire experience. My friend Dena Nance and I have made both the upstairs and downstairs bars at Red Pony our own over the past few years, and now we're learning our way to the luxe black bar in Cork & Cow. The bartenders know us, and on a given evening, we know plenty of the crowd as well.

One of the things that always keeps patrons coming back, you must know, is the effective way both restaurants make use of local and regional distilleries and microdistilleries; here, Corsair Artisan's amazing gin (if you like citrus and juniper, it's for you) and the classic Tennessee whiskey of George Dickel—both recipes from Cork & Cow mixologist Chris Capaldi.

Green Means Go

1½ ounces Corsair Artisan Gin
¾ ounce Strega
½ ounce basil grapefruit syrup (recipe below)
½ ounce fresh lime juice
Sprig of fresh rosemary for garnish

Add ingredients to shaker with ice. Shake and strain into ice-filled double old-fashioned glass. Drop rosemary in glass for garnish.

Basil Grapefruit Syrup (makes 16 ounces)

16 basil leaves
Zest of 2 grapefruits
1 cup of sugar
1 cup of water

Rinse basil and allow it to dry on a towel.
    Combine grapefruit zest, fresh basil, sugar, and water in a medium saucepan. Bring to a simmer, stirring occasionally. While stirring, press basil against the saucepan. At first sign of a boil, remove from heat and allow syrup to cool.
    Once cooled, strain syrup through a fine-mesh strainer. It will keep refrigerated for up to a month.

Cascade Cooler

1½ ounces George Dickel Tennessee Whiskey
1 ounce Domaine de Canton
½ ounce Marie Brizard Orange Curacao
½ ounce fresh lemon juice
Thick slice of orange peel for garnish

Add ingredients to shaker with ice. Shake and strain into ice-filled double old-fashioned glass. Gently squeeze orange peel over top of the drink to express oils and drop into drink.

Dozen Bakery

(615) 509-9680
DOZEN-NASHVILLE.COM
BAKER/OWNER: CLAIRE MENEELY

Over the past several years, a collection of independent bakeries have appeared in the area. Perhaps unsurprisingly, most of them work in the cupcake oeuvre; Claire Meneely, however, got us hooked on her cookies, then led us down a path to different things.

Unlike many of those who started when she did, she doesn't have a brick-and-mortar shop. Instead, she does custom orders and private events, and she sells at several farmers' markets, working from her commercial kitchen. I discovered her at the Franklin Farmers' Market, where she quickly got me hooked on ginger and peanut butter cookies. Everything is made with organic, often local, ingredients. You don't often find cookies this incredibly good, at least not here in the US, where we tend toward accepting prepackaged supermarket cookies as the norm.

These days, people line up, phone, and e-mail to order baked goods of every description, most not realizing the level of training and commitment Claire has put into her business. She graduated from California Culinary Academy's baking and pastry arts program in 2002, then remained and worked in the San Francisco area, refining

her talents. In 2008 she relocated to Paris to study the art of baking under some of the world's masters. She returned to Nashville in 2009, started Dozen, and proceeded to change our sweet palates dramatically for the better.

This is Claire's take on the Southern strawberry shortcake tradition, which can be made year-round to pair with the fruits in season or with fresh jam.

Brown Sugar Shortcakes

(MAKES 12 2-INCH SHORTCAKES)

1 teaspoon vanilla
1 cup cream
2½ cups flour
¾ cup brown sugar
¾ teaspoon salt
1 tablespoon plus 1 teaspoon baking powder
1 stick (½ cup) unsalted butter, cold and
    chopped in small pieces
Melted butter, for brushing on top
Sugar, for sprinkling

Preheat oven to 350°F.

Add the vanilla to the cream.

Place the flour, brown sugar, salt, and baking powder in a bowl and whisk to combine. Use a pastry cutter or rub the mixture between your fingers to blend the cold butter into the flour until it resembles coarse meal.

Slowly add cream mixture while stirring until dough just comes together.

Roll out dough 1 inch thick on floured surface. Use a biscuit cutter to cut out shortcakes.*

Brush tops with melted butter, then sprinkle with sugar. Place on a tray and bake for 15 minutes, until golden brown.

Serve with homemade whipped cream and seasonal fruit and jams from the farmers' market for a delicious dessert—great with strawberries, grilled peaches, blueberries, stewed apples, or whatever is in season!

*Note: Shortcakes will stand straightest if refrigerated overnight before baking.

FRANKLIN FARMERS' MARKET

We're lucky to have an abundance of neighborhood farmers' markets in Nashville, with more sprouting up each year. One of the most longstanding, the Franklin Farmers' Market, formed as a 501(c)(5) in 2002 and has flourished into a large Saturday market with a genuine commitment to local growers and their produce. Held in the parking lot and shed behind the Factory at Franklin, the market serves residents of the county and those who drive from surrounding areas.

I live not far from the Franklin Farmers' Market, and a large percentage of my husband's and my food dollars is spent here. There are no resellers, plenty of reliable farmers, and there's even a winter market that runs from November to March, ensuring that what's available during Tennessee's long growing season (the past few years, we've gotten fresh tomatoes into November, no hothouse required) reaches the consumer. It's also the spot for many CSA pickups.

Besides produce, we can get local organic meats, eggs, handmade cheeses, breads, honey, plants from area nursery farmers, and non-homogenized milk from grass-fed cows via nearby College Grove, Tennessee's wonderful Hatcher Dairy. With the addition of food vendors, live music, and plenty of local craftspeople during spring, summer, and fall, it's a weekly event everyone in Williamson County who cares about what they're eating doesn't want to miss.

Learn more at franklinfarmersmarket.com.

1808 Grille

1808 West End Avenue (Hutton Hotel), West End
(615) 340-0012
1808grille.com
Chef: Charles Phillips

Set as it is on West End, 1808 Grille is a prime spot for business dining and for travelers, but it's also the kind of place locals frequent for its bold menu and tremendously welcoming atmosphere. The sleek, modern restaurant interior set right off the hotel atrium very much keeps with the vibe of the concept hotel: contemporary elegance at an understated best.

But while lovely, it's still about the power of the menu. The magic of Chef Charles has a good deal to do with why we keep coming back. The 1808 Burger is a citywide favorite, and the meat-'n-three concept that focuses on three seasonal, local, farm-to-table sides each day, served with your choice of arctic char, flatiron steak, or Ashley's Farm Chicken Breast, combines the best Southern traditions with the kind of New American style that defines Chef Charles and makes for a seriously popular lunch.

As I wrote this, Chef Charles was really looking forward to cooking with peaches—a Tennessee staple in summer.

"I get excited over peaches; I admit it," he says. "While I'm tempted to try one of the early imposters on the shelf at the store, I exercise some self-discipline and hold out for the magic in season . . . The peach holds down a lead spot in our large plate category. Remember, sourcing great product is 90 percent of a perfect meal, so hit up the local markets, and don't be afraid to ask for a taste—most folks are happy to provide a 'teaser' to close the deal."

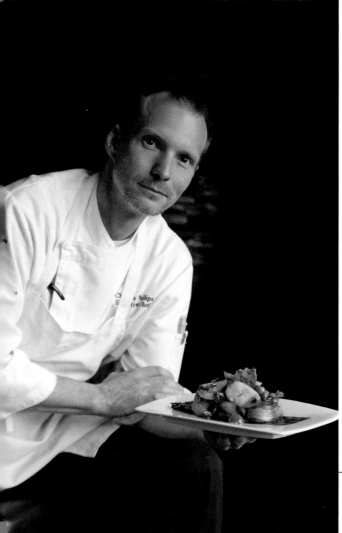

Pork Tenderloin with Peach Salad, Shaved Radicchio & Sweet Cherry Gastrique

(SERVES 4)

For the pork:

2 pork tenderloins
Marinade or dry rub of your choice

For the peach salad:

4 peaches, cut in half
⅓ cup olive oil
¼ cup small-torn pieces of basil (scissors work well)
¼ cup chopped Italian parsley
½ cup toasted pistachios
Salt and fresh ground pepper to taste
Juice of 1 lemon
1 head radicchio

For the cherry gastrique sauce:

1 cup dried cherries
1 cup frozen cherries
1 cup sherry
½ cup vegetable stock
¼ cup sugar

To prepare the pork: Peel the silver skin off the tenderloin and marinate or use a dry rub. This is space to be creative. You can simply chop some herbs, mix with vegetable oil, and marinate, or use some of your favorite grilling spice.*

After the pork has marinated for a couple hours, brush off the excess rub or marinade and place it on an outdoor grill at medium heat.

Slow-cook the pork until it is to your liking, but we suggest cooking it to medium well, 160°F internal temperature.

*Note: Wrapping the pork in bacon is also an option.

To make the peach salad: Lightly oil the peach halves and give a quick sear on high heat on an outdoor grill or a nonstick pan indoors. The idea is to caramelize a bit of the natural sugar without cooking the peach. It must remain crisp, not turn mushy.

Cut the peach half in half again. Toss the peaches with the herbs, oil, pistachio, salt, pepper, and lemon juice to taste. Slice the radicchio very thin and toss everything together.

To make the cherry gastrique sauce: Combine all the listed ingredients in a sauce pot and reduce to a syrup consistency. Place in a blender and puree until very smooth.

To serve: With a pastry brush, "paint" a heavy line of cherry gastrique sauce across the plate. Place a small amount of the peach salad in the center of the plate. Slice the pork into 1-inch medallions and place 3 slices on top of the salad. (Allow pork to rest a few minutes before cutting.)

THE COCKTAILS

"May in Tennessee means horse racing season," says Chef Charles. He's right—not only are we horse country, but beyond the usual first weekend Kentucky Derby, we have our own tradition: The second Saturday in May, we head out to the Iroquois Steeplechase in Belle Meade, named in honor of the great champion of the local Belle Meade line.

With that in mind, lest you think all juleps are out of Kentucky, here are two variations on a classic racing cocktail made with Tennessee whiskey.

Tennessee Julep

½ ounce simple syrup
Small handful of fresh mint leaves
1½ ounces Prichard's Sweet Lucy Liqueur
Soda water

Make the simple syrup by mixing 2 parts sugar with 1 part water. Bring the water to a boil, add sugar, and dissolve, stirring constantly. Allow to cool and store extra in a squeeze bottle in the refrigerator for easy use.

Muddle mint leaves and simple syrup in an empty double old-fashioned glass. Add ice and Sweet Lucy Liqueur. Finish with a splash of soda.

Prefer a sweeter cocktail? Before serving, rim the glass with sugar.

West End Julep

Small handful of fresh mint leaves
1 ounce Bitter Truth Apricot Liqueur
2 ounces Prichard's Tennessee Whiskey
Soda water

Muddle mint and Bitter Truth Apricot Liqueur in an empty highball glass. Add ice and Prichard's whiskey. Finish with a splash of soda.

Find Prichard's products through your local distributor; for more information visit www .prichardsdistillery.com.

8th and Roast

2108 8th Avenue South, Antiques District
(615) 730-8074
facebook.com/roastinc
Owners: Brad and Lesa Wood

Coffee culture in Nashville has often seemed heavily focused in East Nashville, Hillsboro/Belmont, or over in the 12South neighborhood, but the 2012 move and expansion of Roast, Inc., brought one of the best and most dedicated coffee companies to 8th Avenue South and the Antiques District— and brought better-than-fair-trade coffees that are truly excellent, whether you want a cup of black or something with a few more ingredients. What they do is coffee, and they do it right.

This is relevant because we drink a whole lot of coffee, large expansive city that we are. We hang out in lots of coffee shops. I interview people in coffee shops, to the point that a couple feel like extended offices to me.

Owner Lesa Wood is generally roasting husband Brad's carefully sourced beans in the back, while the baristas brew up front. Set in a 1930s building, there's an attractive wall of raw brick, set with vintage-looking lights.

The recent addition of amazing baked goods, sweet and savory, by Gina Olds of Flour, Sugar, Eggs, complete the coffee shop's offerings. Her buttery croissants, rich quiche, and delectable frittatas make a divine culinary impact. The glorious scents of coffee and warm croissants wafting through the air create a small paradise on 8th Avenue South.

Vanilla Bean Café Au Lait

(MAKES 1 DRINK)

And, of course, you can't have a coffee shop without a little café au lait.

¼ teaspoon vanilla bean paste*
1 tablespoon sweetened condensed milk
6 ounces milk (can be regular or milk substitute such as almond milk)
6 ounces fresh-brewed coffee
Sprinkle of cinnamon

Mix the vanilla bean paste and sweetened condensed milk together in your mug. Warm milk on the stove top to approximately 140°F. This will be steamy milk, but be careful not to scald. Add brewed coffee to your mug and stir to mix. Add warm milk to mug.

Garnish with a sprinkle of cinnamon. There are many versions of this drink; we also love substituting caramel, agave syrup, or honey for the vanilla bean paste.

*Note: Vanilla bean paste is recommended over liquid extract because of the alcohol taste that is released from liquid when it's added to the hot coffee.

Mini Spinach Feta Frittata

(MAKES 6 FRITTATAS)

Butter
12 large eggs
¾ cup whole milk
¾ teaspoon freshly ground black pepper
½ teaspoon salt
8 ounces fresh spinach, coarsely chopped
8 ounces crumbled feta
3 tablespoons chopped fresh parsley

Preheat oven to 375°F. Generously butter 6 muffin cups.

Whisk the eggs, milk, pepper, and salt in a large bowl until blended.

Divide the spinach and feta evenly in the prepared muffin cups. Fill cups with egg mixture and gently stir, mixing all the ingredients together. Top with chopped parsley.

Bake until the frittatas puff and are just set in the center, about 10–15 minutes.

Using a rubber spatula, loosen the frittatas from the muffin cups and slide them onto a platter.

ETCH

303 DEMONBREUN STREET, DOWNTOWN
(615) 522-0685
ETCHRESTAURANT.COM
EXECUTIVE CHEF/OWNER: DEB PAQUETTE
PASTRY CHEF: MEGAN WILLIAMS
SOUS CHEF/SALADS: KENJI NAKAGAWA

Chef Deb Paquette is nothing short of a Nashville legend—a graduate of the Culinary Institute of America, she's best known for the many years she and husband Ernie spent as owners of Zola restaurant, winning national and local awards for the incredible fare Deb magically brought to life. When Zola closed, the city collectively mourned, as Chef Deb and Ernie took off for the Caribbean before the owners of a popular Italian restaurant wooed them back with an offer Deb couldn't refuse.

In short, they gave her the opportunity to create a signature restaurant in the Encore building. While the build-out happened, Deb served as consultant to 12South's Urban Grub restaurant and helped Jeff and Jenny Pennington develop their exquisite microdistillery product, Whisper Creek. Already having a fine reputation as a consultant, everything she touched developed significant buzz and made the excitement for Etch even stronger.

In 2012 Etch came beautifully together, on the ground floor of the Encore tower. The space provides a private dining room, bar, and an open kitchen with bar-style seating so you can interact directly with the chef and her kitchen (and she's a joy to watch—they all are).

The menu is creative and diverse, changing seasonally. A sampling of Deb's menu might have you contemplating starters like Chinese braised pork or octopus and shrimp bruschetta; the Etch Salad offers up fennel, green apple, arugula, radicchio, blue cheese, hazelnuts, and a champagne vinaigrette. For an entree, you might consider the pork tenderloin or the Moroccan spiced venison.

The following recipe can be used for that spiced venison as well as for duck breast, depending on your preference. "This dish has many components," Deb tells me, "but all very easy and fun."

ETCH DUCK BREAST WITH GINGER GRITS, SWEET POTATO GUAVA SCHMEAR, CRANBERRY RELISH & PEAR BUTTER

(SERVES 6–8)

Venison may easily be substituted for duck in this recipe. Where noted, some of these steps can be done a day in advance for ease of preparation.

SPICE FOR MEAT

This spice is called *Ras el hanout,* which, according to Deb, means "head of the shop" or "don't touch your mama's spice."

1 tablespoon cumin seed

1 tablespoon fennel seed

2 tablespoons coriander seed

1 teaspoon ground ginger

1 teaspoon cinnamon

1 teaspoon black pepper

1 teaspoon turmeric

¼ teaspoon nutmeg

¼ teaspoon ground clove

¼ teaspoon allspice

1 teaspoon cayenne

1 teaspoon cardamom

2 tablespoons sugar

1 tablespoon kosher salt

Grind seeds to a fine powder. Mix all the ingredients together well and store in a jar.

Duck Breast or Venison

4 large duck moulard (double breasts) or one per person if using small breasts or 1½ pounds venison

If there is a lot of fat on the duck, remove a layer to not have more than ¼ inch. Score fat, being careful not to cut the meat. Place breast fat-side down on a metal pan and freeze until fat is firm. Lightly salt breast and sear fat-side down in a low-heated sauté pan to help render fat. (Do not brown.) Cool and put in fridge. A half hour before grilling, season generously with the spice mixture and let sit at room temperature. Grill carefully to avoid burning your spices and reach a nice medium-rare temperature. Let sit 10 minutes before slicing.

GINGER GRITS

1 quart water

1 stick (½ cup) butter

1 teaspoon salt

1 teaspoon black pepper

1¾ cups stone-ground grits

½ cup candied ginger (choose the syrupy type)

Fresh grated ginger to taste, if desired

Boil water with butter, salt, and black pepper. Stir in grits with a whisk. Cook on low heat till thick, about 20 minutes. If too thick, add a bit of water. If too thin, add a touch more grits.

When grits no longer have their rawness, add ½ cup candied ginger. If you want more sweetness and ginger flavor, add a bit more candied ginger, or add fresh grated for more of a bite.

Hold warm until ready to serve.

SWEET POTATO GUAVA SCHMEAR

2 pounds sweet potatoes
2–3 ounces guava paste
4–6 tablespoons unsalted butter
Pinch of salt

Roast the sweet potatoes at 350° until soft, about ½ hour; or poke with a fork to vent then microwave 10 minutes, turning after 5 minutes.

Peel the potatoes when warm and place in a food processor with guava paste and butter. Puree until it reaches a baby food consistency. Add a pinch of salt.

This can be made ahead of time and reheated in the microwave or served room temperature.

CRANBERRY RELISH

(MAKES 12 OUNCES)

3 cups frozen cranberries
½ cup sugar
1 tablespoon sumac (found at Middle Eastern grocery stores or international markets)
Juice and zest of 1 lime
½ teaspoon salt
1 serrano pepper, seeds removed and chopped
½ cup walnut oil
½ teaspoon toasted cumin seeds, ground
½ bunch cilantro, chopped

Place all the ingredients except the cilantro in a food processor. Pulse until berries are broken up into bits. Do *not* puree. Add chopped cilantro.

This can be made a day in advance. Leftovers are wonderful on toast or sweet potatoes.

PEAR BUTTER

(MAKES 16 OUNCES)

4 sticks (2 cups) butter
½ cup pear liqueur (Mathilde preferred)
½ cup pear puree
½ teaspoon cayenne
Pinch of salt
2 tablespoons sugar

Dice up the butter and put in a mixer. Slowly begin to whip the butter, then slowly add pear liqueur and pear puree and allow to emulsify. Add cayenne, salt, and sugar and whip till fluffy.

Put in an airtight container and refrigerate until needed, but pull out in time to soften a bit before serving. (Save extra for your morning bagel!)

BANANA FUN DOTS

1 ripe banana
½ teaspoon turmeric
1 teaspoon sugar
¼ cup walnut oil
¼ cup water

Place all the ingredients in a blender and puree till smooth. Transfer to a squirt bottle.

Plating the dish: Put a nice big schmear of sweet potato puree on the plate. Place a scoop of grits on the schmear. Place sliced grilled duck around the grits. Add 2 teaspoons pear butter to grits, flowing onto duck, or set it on the table and let guests plop it on themselves. Add about 1 tablespoon cranberry relish to the side of the grits. Squirt banana dots around the plate to garnish. Some nice greens poking out of the grits is a fabulous touch.

Tuna, Eggplant & Spinach Ponzu Salad

(SERVES 4–6)

Zola, Chef Deb Paquette's previous restaurant, which she closed a few years ago after thirteen years at the top of Nashville's dining scene, had a reputation for outstanding salads. Her new location, Etch, is building a similar reputation, in part due to the original thinking of Sous Chef Kenji Nakagawa. Like other recipes Paquette contributed to this book, it's a multistep process, but many pieces can be created in advance, and none of them are terribly complicated. The real priority is getting the right ingredients, like Chinese or Japanese eggplant and really good tuna from your fishmonger.

For the marinated eggplant:

3 pounds Chinese or Japanese eggplant
Enough cannola or peanut oil for frying
10 ounces citrus vinegar
1¼ cups soy sauce
½ cup rice vinegar
½ cup sugar
2 ounces water
1 ounce mushroom soy sauce
1 ounce oyster sauce
1 teaspoon minced ginger

For the ponzu vinaigrette:
(Make in advance and put in fridge to allow flavors to develop.)
6 ounces citrus seasoning (available at Asian markets)
5 ounces soy sauce
3 ounces rice vinegar
3 tablespoons sugar
2 ounces sake
1½ ounces water
½ teaspoon Coleman's mustard
1 tablespoon lemon juice
1 tablespoon lime juice
2 teaspoons fresh ginger
1 cup canola oil
¼ cup sesame oil

For the spiced tuna:

1 tablespoon red pepper flakes
¼ cup fennel seed
3 tablespoons paprika
2 tablespoons salt
12–18 ounces quality tuna (2–3 ounces per person)
Sesame oil for coating tuna

For the salad:

½ cup daikon, cut in small pieces
1 brick smoked tofu, cut in small pieces
3 ounces thinly sliced button mushrooms
5 spring onions, sliced on the bias
About 2 pounds fresh spinach (5–6 ounces per person)
Optional additions: cilantro, broccoli, sprouts
Red bell pepper slivers for garnish

To prepare the eggplant: Cut the stems off and cut the eggplant into quarters. Cut each quarter into 3- to 4-inch pieces.

Use a fryer or heat 2 inches of oil in a wide pot or skillet. Bring the oil temperature to 350°F. Meanwhile, place a 2-quart pot of water on the stove and bring to a boil.

Deep-fry the eggplant for 30–45 seconds until it turns bright purple and softens (you may need to do this in batches). Drain well. When all is

fried, place the eggplant into boiling water for 10 seconds. Shock it in ice water and drain. Place a towel on a sheet pan and set eggplant to dry. Let dry for 1 hour before placing in marinade.

Mix the marinade ingredients (citrus vinegar, soy sauce, rice vinegar, sugar, water, mushroom soy sauce, oyster sauce, and minced ginger) in a bowl and whisk to blend. Pour over the eggplant in a shallow dish. Place a plate on top to hold the eggplant down in the marinade. Marinate for at least 2 hours; overnight is fine. The marinade is good for 3–4 days.

To make the vinaigrette: Blend all the ingredients at high speed in a blender for 1 minute. It will look foamy at first, but quickly settle down.

To prepare the tuna: Grind the red pepper flakes, fennel seed, and paprika. Place in a bowl, add the salt, and mix well.

Cut the tuna into 6 x 3-inch pieces. Slather with a light coating of sesame oil, then generously coat tuna with spice mix. Add the spice to the fish, not the fish to the bowl, so you don't contaminate the spice mix if you have extra.

Set your sauté pan on medium heat with oil covering the bottom of the pan. Heat each side of the tuna so all sides get ⅛ to ¼ inch of cooking. Cool the tuna, then refrigerate to rest for at least 1 hour.

To assemble: Toss all the salad ingredients with 3–4 ounces of ponzu vinaigrette (shake well first).

Plate onto individual plates and top with thin, chilled slices of the tuna and eggplant. Toss red bell pepper for color.

Flourless Chocolate Cake with Coffee Crème Brûlée, Milk Chocolate Crumble & Mocha Mousse

There are few desserts on the Etch menu that limit themselves to a single flavor component—instead, when you visit, expect layered flavors that make your mouth celebrate the combinations. The flourless aspect of this particular recipe makes it a good selection for those on a gluten-free diet. But like most true gastronomic dessert delights, the calorie count might mean a few extra crunches in the morning for the health conscious—because skipping it isn't an option. (Note: It's best to use a reliable food scale for this recipe.)

(SERVES 8–10)

For the chocolate cake:

8 ounces (1 cup) dark chocolate (55% cocoa
    solids or higher)
3 ounces (6 tablespoons) butter
Pinch of salt
½ teaspoon vanilla extract
2 eggs
1 egg yolk
1 tablespoon sugar

For the coffee crème brûlée:

1 ounce (2 tablespoons) coffee
10 ounces (1 cup plus 2 tablespoons) cream
1½ ounces (3 tablespoons) sugar
1½ sheets gelatin, bloomed
3 egg yolks
1 teaspoon espresso powder

For the milk chocolate crumble:

4½ ounces (1 tablespoon) milk powder, divided
3 ounces (¼ cup plus 2 tablespoons) cocoa powder
½ ounce (1 tablespoon) cornstarch
2 ounces (¼ cup) rice flour
2 ounces (¼ cup) sugar
½ ounce (1 tablespoon) salt
4 ounces (½ cup) butter, melted
5 ounces (½ cup plus 2 tablespoons)
    milk chocolate, melted

For the mocha mousse:

2 tablespoons water
2½ ounces (¼ cup plus 1 tablespoon) sugar
21½ ounces cream, divided (5½ ounces hot)
6 egg yolks
1½ sheets gelatin, bloomed
9 ounces (1 cup plus 2 tablespoons)
    dark chocolate (55% cocoa solids or higher)
¼ teaspoon salt
2 teaspoons coffee extract

FIDO

1812 21st Avenue South, Hillsboro Village
(615) 777-3436
FIDOCAFE.COM
Chef: John Stephenson
Head Baker: Lisa Bachman Jones
Owner: Bob Bernstein

FIDO has been around for more than a decade now, one of the several cafes under the umbrella of owner and coffee roaster Bob Bernstein. We might have come late to the coffee revolution as a city—only in the past few years has the locally roasted coffee thing really exploded—but Bob has been on this path since at least 1993, when he opened Bongo Java, his first cafe and roasting house offering fair trade or better coffees roasted right here (why, yes, you can buy it online). A commitment to sustainability means FIDO, which is as much restaurant as coffee business for Bernstein, makes use of plenty of local and organic foods where they can.

FIDO is usually filled with Vanderbilt or Belmont students, along with businesspeople taking a break and advantage of the Wi-Fi as well as slurping down excellent coffee.

There's a fine menu of salads, sandwiches, omelets (breakfast served all day), and more, thanks to the dedicated work of Chef John Stephenson. I met John when he was dating his gorgeous baker wife, Katherine, who baked for FIDO for a time. These days Lisa Bachman Jones does those honors, and the baked goods in the glass case as you wait in line to order are completely irresistible, from homemade cookies to rich chocolate zucchini cake.

The pumpkin chocolate-chip muffins here are more than worth the effort if you want to really impress your guests.

THE PC MUFFIN

(MAKES 10 LARGE MUFFINS)

½ cup sugar

½ cup packed brown sugar

½ cup canola oil

½ cup olive oil

½ cup unsweetened applesauce

1¾ cups canned pumpkin

3 eggs

3½ cups flour

2 teaspoons cinnamon

1 teaspoon cloves

1 teaspoon nutmeg

1½ teaspoons baking soda

1½ teaspoons baking powder

1 teaspoon salt

1½ cups chocolate chips

Preheat oven to 275°F.

Combine the sugars, oils, applesauce, pumpkin, and eggs in a mixer with a paddle attachment on the middle speed or whisk by hand at a rapid rate until all the ingredients are evenly mixed.

In a separate bowl, combine the remaining dry ingredients. Turn the mixer off and add dry ingredients to the wet ingredients. Blend on a low speed or by hand with a whisk until evenly mixed.

Spray a muffin tin with Baker's Joy or use muffin papers. Use a spoon to place approximately ¾ cup of batter into each muffin cup. Bake for about 30 minutes, rotating the pan after 15 minutes.

Use a toothpick to check the muffins. If the toothpick comes out clean, the muffins are done; if it has batter stuck to it, the muffins need about 5 more minutes.

55 SOUTH

403 MAIN STREET, FRANKLIN
(615) 538-6001
EAT55SOUTH.COM
CHEF: CARL SCHULTHEIS
EXECUTIVE CHEF/OWNER: JASON MCCONNELL

My husband and I have spent many a Sunday morning at 55 South, partaking of brunch. Let me just say that the French toast (Pecan Pain Perdu) here is among the best—and one of my personal comfort foods. Of course, there's plenty on the brunch menu to love, including the Fried Pork Chop Sandwich, with avocado and hot sauce, the NOLA Omelet, or maybe the 55 Wedge with blue cheese dressing (pretty classic Nashville, the iceberg wedge salad).

The bar is a regular draw, not just for Sunday Bloody Marys, but after work on a weekday, when the whole of Franklin converges to shoot oysters, visit with friends, and sip on the happy hour specials. My best friend, Jennifer Matthews, and I have sat at the sidewalk patio regularly, consuming house-made sangria.

Folks love 55 South for oysters and whiskey (including the distilleries of Tennessee and Kentucky). The menu concept showcases the cuisine you find when you drive I-55 south from Memphis down to New Orleans, with a little Nashville for good measure. From the pork chop mentioned earlier to gumbo and jambalaya, there's a little Tennessee, a little Mississippi, a bit of Louisiana—there's even a hint of Mexico, including handmade guacamole.

The recipe for Nashville Hot Chicken is Jason's take on pure Nashville, the hot chicken phenomenon (find another take, from Biscuit Love Truck, on page 173). Jason's variation combines a hot rub that will tingle your taste buds (or more, if you up the cayenne content) but that mediates the heat with the classic tang of mayo and the simplicity of white bread—just the way you might with a spicy barbecue sauce (where the mayo would come with the coleslaw).

Firepot Chai

2905 12th Avenue South, Suite 106, 12South
firepotchai.com, facebook.com/firepot-chai
Owner/Brewer: Sarah Scarborough

While coffee seems to be blooming in the South, tea still stands as a little more exotic. Not that we don't have tons of sweet tea around here but, heavens, we make that with tea bags from Lipton and Luzianne. The pleasure of true blended tea is something else entirely. Firepot Chai makes that difference come alive for us.

When Sarah Scarborough began her tea odyssey, her first creation was an amazing chai blend she called Firepot Chai. Rich, deeply spiced, and flavorful, the blend became a huge hit with friends and family and built a longtime customer following.

That continued even as Scarborough went out and created a wide variety of products for other companies, traveling the world from New Zealand to China, learned the ins and outs of the tea world and tea markets. At the time, her goal was producing organic, fair trade and better artisan teas. Now she's returned and settled in Nashville, leaving the corporate tea world behind to focus on the lush chai blend that started it all.

In August 2013 she opened this artisan tea microbrewery in 12South, between Sloco and Burger Up, in one of the city's most in-demand pieces of culinary real estate. Here you'll find Sarah grinding, blending, and brewing teas.

Likewise, instead of offering up Southern sweet tea to pair with the recipes here, let's try a couple of cocktails and even a marinade made with Sarah's international award-winning chai. You can order her incredible chai concentrate directly at firepotchai.com. Trust me, you'll drink the concentrate all by itself if you're a tea lover. Being one myself, to this I can attest.

The Cauveri Cocktail

Truly, bourbon is a Kentucky thing, and whiskey is a Tennessee thing, but we're all for cultural exchanges (and Nashville is so close to the state line). You get a bit of sweetness here from the chai concentrate, a citrus kick from the lime, and added depth from the bitters—it's a terrific alternative to the old-school julep.

2 ounces Kentucky bourbon
1 tablespoon fresh lime juice
1 tablespoon plus 1 teaspoon Firepot
    Chai Concentrate
3 dashes orange bitters
4 ounces soda water

Combine all the ingredients in a glass filled with ice.

Firepot Chai Hot Toddy

It does get cold outside here, and I suspect this cocktail will perk you up if you've got a bit of a cold, too. Bourbon, honey, and water are old Southern prescriptions for sniffles and scratchy throats, but the chai syrup makes that blend taste like Christmas, with its rich spices.

1 ounce Kentucky bourbon
1 tablespoon lemon juice
1 tablespoon Firepot Chai Concentrate
1 teaspoon honey
4 ounces hot water

Combine all the ingredients in a mug and stir till blended.

CHAI FRIED CHICKEN

(SERVES 4)

The chicken needs to marinate for two nights, but the end result is truly worth the wait!
Serve alongside a salad dressed with Firepot Chai Salad Dressing/Marinade (recipe below).

4 chicken breasts or 6 chicken thighs
1 bottle dill pickle juice, pickles removed
5 teaspoons loose-leaf Firepot Black Tea Chai,* divided
2 cups buttermilk
2 cups flour
3 teaspoons baking powder
1 teaspoon salt
Oil for frying

Cover the chicken with pickle juice and soak overnight.

Drain and rinse the chicken. Set aside.

Steep 4 teaspoons of Firepot Black Tea Chai in 2 cups of boiling water for 5 minutes. Strain and cool the chai.

Combine steeped tea with buttermilk. Add chicken and refrigerate for 8 hours or overnight.

Combine flour, 1 teaspoon of Firepot Black Tea Chai, baking powder, and salt. Fill a cast-iron skillet with 1 inch of canola oil. Heat to medium.

Dredge the chicken in the flour mixture and fry in the skillet for about 8 minutes on each side, until done.

*Note: Order Firepot Black Tea Chai from FirePotChai.com or facebook.com/firepot-chai.

FIREPOT CHAI SALAD DRESSING/MARINADE

(MAKES 12 OUNCES)

This marinade works for far more than fried chicken, I like it on pork loin, and if you're a fan of salads topped with meat, use it as a delicious dressing on your greens, or marinate your chicken or salmon in it prior to grilling. The tea and citrus combination pairs beautifully with salmon.

2 teaspoons Firepot Black Tea Chai steeped in
   ½ cup boiling water for 5 minutes
1 cup cold-pressed olive oil
¼ cup apple cider vinegar
2 tablespoons freshly squeezed orange juice
1 tablespoon freshly squeezed lemon juice
1 tablespoon tamari

Combine ingredients in a jar. Cover and chill. Keep refrigerated for up to 1 week.

Flyte World Dining and Wine

718 Division Street, 8th Avenue South, The Gulch
(615) 255-6200
FLYTENASHVILLE.COM
Chef: Matthew Lackey
Owners: Scott Sears and Scott Atkinson

Flyte World Dining and Wine rests at the far edge of The Gulch, across the street from Arnold's, next door to one of the city's favorite wine and liquor emporiums, just before you hit the new Convention Center along 8th Avenue South. When Scott Sears and Scott Atkinson opened the restaurant in 2007, the almost immediate recession meant restaurants closing left and right. Flyte, with its signature flytes of extraordinary wine, tapas in the bar, and marvelous inventive menu, proved a powerhouse survivor.

The best recent development for Flyte has been the arrival of Chef Matthew Lackey, a native of Sumner County trained at the Culinary Institute of America and Le Cordon Bleu College of Culinary Arts, a part-time farmer and veteran of some of the best kitchens in Nashville and Charleston.

As a native of Castilian Springs, just north of the city, Lackey knows the traditional Middle Tennessee palate well and ignores the larger, outside food world's trends to focus on real local food done the way he knows it. "We're not going to mold the 'local' into something that's not us," he says decisively.

Brought up on his family's farm in Castilian Springs, just outside Music City, he returned to his roots when his grandfather was in his final illness and opted to stay and see that farm revitalized. Today he grows crops that in turn help supply the restaurant, in addition to working with local mainstay farmers like the iconic Farmer Dave to keeps Flyte's kitchens brimming.

The dish he's provided may seem on the exotic side, but it's delicious, as Flyte patrons know. Lackey plays on the notion of chicken and waffles and the traditional bacon and waffles and creates something distinct.

"We serve this with a buttermilk panna cotta," he says, "but that isn't practical for a home cook, so I've given you my buttermilk dressing recipe to pair with it." The pig ears have a chewy porkiness, without bacon's smoky flavor. "Try 'em, you'll love 'em," smiles Lackey.

PIG EARS WITH WAFFLES

(SERVES 6–8)

A scale is critical to achieve correct proportions for the waffles.

For the yeasted waffles:

340 grams whole milk (Lackey sources from
    Hatcher Dairy, a local non-homogenized source.)
4 grams sugar
7 grams instant yeast
84 grams butter (82% fat)
2 farm eggs
50 grams grade A maple syrup
240 grams White Lily all-purpose flour
3 grams salt

For the buttermilk dressing:

160 grams buttermilk (Lackey sources from
    local Cruz Family Dairy.)
72 grams crème fraîche
44 grams mayonnaise (Duke's preferred)
6 grams togarashi (a Japanese hot pepper staple
    available at Asian grocery stores and in some
    supermarkets in the ethnic foods section)
1½ grams salt
1 gram black pepper

For the pig ears:

500 grams pig ears (available from your butcher)
250 grams pork stock
2 grams salt
10 grams Tabasco or your favorite hot sauce

To make the waffles: Heat milk to 106°F (using a
thermometer), then add the sugar and remove
from heat. Add the instant yeast and allow this
yeast starter to rest for 20 minutes.

Melt the butter.

Lightly fold the eggs, maple syrup, and flour
together until they are incorporated. Then fold in
the yeast starter from above.

Finish by lightly folding in the salt. Cover the bowl
with plastic wrap and allow it to rest for 2 hours.

Spoon the batter into your hot waffle iron, until it
just lightly covers the skillet. Cook all the batter
and reserve the waffles in a warm oven until
ready to serve.

To make the dressing: Thoroughly whisk all the
ingredients together in a bowl. Refrigerate while
the waffles cook.

To prepare the pig ears: Place all the ingredients
except hot sauce in a pressure cooker set to high
and cook for 50 minutes.

When finished, release pressure and lay the ears
out in a single layer. Allow them to cool, then cut
the ears into ½-inch strips.

Fry the ears at 360°F until they are golden brown.
Toss in a bowl with your favorite hot sauce.

To assemble the dish: Set some pig ears atop
a waffle on a plate, and drizzle with buttermilk
dressing.

F. Scott's Restaurant & Jazz Bar

2210 Crestmore Road, Green Hills
(615) 269-5861
FSCOTTS.COM
Executive Chef: Kevin Ramquist
Owners: Wendy Holcomb Burch and Elise Loehr

F. Scott's (as in "Fitzgerald"—note the jazz theme) has been a Nashville mainstay for thirty years, back when the notion of locally owned restaurants was frequently scoffed at by area residents. The place has weathered the test of time and gone through a long list of talented owners, managers, and chefs over the years. These days, powerhouse owners Wendy Burch and Elise Loehr continue to confirm the restaurant's place in the firmament of iconic Nashville fine-dining establishments.

I first started visiting F. Scott's with my parents, back when I was in grad school and home for visits. We'd sit in the bar, drink wine, and listen to live jazz from local artists like favorite Beegie Adair. F. Scott's remains the place to go for the jazz and the whole picture of a great night out, from the entertainment to meal, across age demographics.

Chef Kevin Ramquist and his sous chefs have a very fresh ingredient-focused menu and make every effort to support local farmers where possible. Any of the house-made salads emphasize those points, to be sure.

The offering of fresh local Hereford beef, grilled to your liking, really makes a positive impression on diners, but there's plenty on the menu for those who don't fancy beef,

including an ever-changing vegetarian plate made with whatever is freshest and in season. Starters include excellent razor clams and really lovely, creamy onion soup, at least at this writing, since this is a menu that changes at will with the seasons. Don't forget the wine list—F. Scott's was one of the first places in town to serve really good wines by the glass, and they keep up the tradition solidly.

Sweet Potato Gnocchi with Spiced Parmesan Cream

(SERVES 4–6)

A note from the chef: Sweet Potato Gnocchi with Spiced Parmesan Cream is great alone or with almost anything—duck, fish, vegetables—the possibilities are endless; just have fun with it, bon appétit!

2 large sweet potatoes (about 2 pounds)
¼ cup canola oil
¾ cup ricotta cheese
½ cup finely grated Parmesan cheese
1¼ cups sifted all-purpose flour, plus some for dusting and floured surface (about ¼ cup)
1 tablespoon brown sugar
1 teaspoon salt
Pinch of nutmeg
1 tablespoon butter
2 cups Spiced Parmesan Cream (recipe below)

Preheat oven to 350°F.

Peel and rinse sweet potatoes and cut lengthwise into medium-size chunks. Toss in canola oil to coat the potatoes, then place on a sheet tray and bake until cooked through, 30–45 minutes.

Place potatoes in a bowl and mash until smooth with a fork or potato masher. Stir in ricotta and Parmesan cheese, then add flour, brown sugar, salt, and nutmeg. Mix well with hands until a dough ball forms (add more flour if your dough seems loose; it should still be a bit sticky).

Place the dough on a flat, floured surface and cut into 4 pieces. Wrap each piece of dough in plastic wrap and place in the refrigerator to cool for about 15–20 minutes.

After the dough has cooled, take it out of the refrigerator and remove plastic wrap. Using your hands, roll each dough piece into a long tube or rope shape about ¾ inch in diameter. Dust with flour as needed to keep the dough from sticking to your hands or the table. Cut the tubes into 1½-inch pieces and set the formed gnocchi on a sheet tray covered in flour.

Bring a large pot of salted water to a boil, then turn heat down to medium-high and add gnocchi until they float (about 1 minute). Toss the gnocchi in a little olive oil and place in the refrigerator until ready to use.

To serve: In a large pan, melt butter over medium-high heat. Add the gnocchi and brown all over. Once browned, add the Spiced Parmesan Cream and lightly stir until the gnocchi and cream are heated through and sauce coats the back of a spoon. Serve!

Spiced Parmesan Cream

(MAKES ABOUT 1 QUART)

1 cup white wine
1 quart heavy cream
¾ cup grated Parmesan cheese
1 teaspoon allspice
Salt and pepper to taste

In a medium saucepan over medium-high heat, add white wine and reduce by over a half. (Keep an eye on this to make sure it does not reduce too much or burn.)

Add heavy cream, Parmesan cheese, and allspice and cook for 10 minutes. Remove from heat, and add salt and pepper to taste.

The Grilled Cheeserie
Gourmet Grilled Cheese Truck

315 10th Avenue North (commissary kitchen)
(615) 491-9640
For daily location updates, visit facebook.com/GrilledCheeserie
or thegrilledcheeserietruck.com
Chef: Crystal De Luna-Bogan
Owners: Crystal De Luna-Bogan and Joseph Bogan

One of the favorite food trucks to arrive on the scene in recent years is the Grilled Cheeserie. Working on the theory that there's really nothing as soothing and comfort-inducing as a really good grilled cheese sandwich, Crystal De Luna-Bogan has turned that sandwich into something of an art form. Now, wherever the truck parks, you'll see lines forming and smiles on faces.

The concept works in part because Crystal uses artisan products, among them Sweetwater Valley cheddar from East Tennessee (you can buy it online at sweetwatervalley.com) and fresh bread made by Silke's Old World Breads, a local baker (this too can be ordered, at silkesoldworldbreads.com). The addition of Benton's Bacon, another Tennessee artisan icon, really just makes for perfection.

If you prefer to buy local, Crystal says you can absolutely find artisan breads and cheeses in your own region. But the secret to a really delicious sandwich is taking that step from prepackaged, processed cheese and bread from the local mega-mart and moving toward food made fresh and perfectly from artisan sources. You'll support your small business owners and in the process get something tantalizing and delicious.

Along with the sandwich comes the Grilled Cheeserie's apple and onion jam, which combines with it to make the most brilliant comfort food you've ever tasted. This is heaven. Now serve it up with the tomato soup recipe here and every rainy day will fly by unnoticed.

GRILLED CHEESE

(MAKES 8 SANDWICHES)

1 cup butter, softened

1 loaf Silke's Seeded Multigrain Bread (or your local artisan multigrain)

8–10 slices Sweetwater Valley Buttermilk Cheddar (or your local artisan cheddar)

1 cup (more if desired) Caramelized Apple & Onion Jam (recipe on next page)

16–20 slices Benton's Bacon (or other smoky bacon of your choice), baked in 350°F oven on a sheet tray for 15–20 minutes

Preheat a skillet over medium heat.

For each sandwich, generously butter both sides of a slice of multigrain bread. Place bread onto skillet and add a slice of cheese. Top with desired amount of apple and onion jam and 2–3 slices bacon. Butter a second slice of bread on both sides and place on top of sandwich.

Grill until lightly browned and flip over; continue grilling until cheese is melted. Repeat with remaining bread and cheese to complete your sandwiches.

Caramelized Apple & Onion Jam

(MAKES ABOUT 1 CUP, ENOUGH FOR 4–6 SANDWICHES)

2 tablespoons butter, divided

2 large onions, small diced

1 cup unfiltered apple cider, preferably
   with no sugar added

1 teaspoon Herbes de Provence

1 tablespoon honey, maybe more depending on the
   sweetness of your apples

2 teaspoons fresh-cracked black peppercorns

2 large organic Fuji apples, medium diced

1 large organic Granny Smith apple, medium diced

1 tablespoon apple pectin

1 teaspoon sea salt

In a heavy-bottomed pot on medium heat, melt
1 tablespoon butter and caramelize the onions,
stirring frequently. Once caramelized, add cider,
herbs, honey, and pepper and let simmer.

In a sauté pan on high heat, melt the rest of the
butter and sauté the apples until browned; you
still want them to have texture. Set aside.

In a small bowl, whisk the pectin with about
¼ cup of water. Set aside.

Puree the onion mixture in the pot with a stick
blender, or use a food processor. Mix until
smooth, then stir in the apples, pectin, and salt.
Let simmer for about 20–30 minutes.

Old-Fashioned Tomato Soup

(MAKES 4–6 8-OUNCE SERVINGS)

Tomato soup just always seems to pair best with a grilled cheese sandwich, and the Grilled
Cheeserie cooks up a monstrously good tomato soup. It relies on the tomatoes and herbs
to give it body and flavor.

1 onion, medium diced

2 tablespoons butter

3 pounds ripe tomatoes or 1 (28-ounce) can
   tomatoes (preferably San Marzano)

1 tablespoon Benton's Bacon fat (or other
   smoky bacon of your choice)

1 teaspoon salt

1 tablespoon freshly ground black pepper

½ cup heavy cream

1 tablespoon sugar

Sweat onions in butter until translucent, then add
tomatoes. Simmer about 1 hour.

Add bacon fat, salt, and pepper, then blend. Add
cream and sugar and simmer on low heat for up
to 2 hours.

Holland House Bar and Refuge

935 Eastland Avenue, East Nashville
(615) 262-4190
HOLLANDHOUSEBARANDREFUGE.COM
Mixologist: Jeremiah Blake
Owners: Terry Raley and Cees Brinkman

Holland House is East Nashville's take on the speakeasy concept, and superbly talented head bartender Jeremiah Blake never ceases to amaze us with his inventive takes on artisan cocktails. The goal of Holland House is simple—a smooth blending of the most creative cocktails with a menu of stylish New American dishes, with constant consideration of the pairing of the two aspects of the restaurant.

The interior is gorgeous and a little retro, with high vaulted ceilings and a pair of maple bars competing for your attention. It's a lovely place to while away an evening. A dinner here is a splendid thing, and no hurried affair. The duck burger is exceptional (well, any take they give a burger tends to be), as is the bistro steak and the chicken leg confit.

But, of course, at Holland House you mustn't fail to order a cocktail, and this one is a real stunner. I particularly like it for its use of the new Belle Meade Bourbon, courtesy of Nelson's Green Brier Distillery—one of the newer microdistillers in the Nashville area. It's a revival of a pre-Prohibition brand once famous in this part of the country, and the guys at Nelson's just happen to be the great-grandsons of the original maker, Charles Nelson.

LISTLESS EASE

2 ounces Belle Meade Bourbon
½ ounce Atsby's Amberthorne Vermouth
½ ounce Chamomile Cordial
12 drops (2 dashes) grapefruit bitters

Stir and serve, topped with a grapefruit peel sliver, expressing the juice along the rim of the glass before dropping it in.

Jasmine

8105 Moores Lane, Brentwood
(615) 661-0169
JASMINENASHVILLE.COM
Chef/Owner: Anuphap
Kornsuwan

If I have a default restaurant at all, it's Jasmine. Set in a shopping plaza in Cool Springs—the rapidly growing space that bridges and merges Franklin and Brentwood in Williamson County—that also houses Publix and Home Depot, it may seem unprepossessing from the outside, but the interior is a welcome respite from suburban sprawl. The decor is simple and Asian with a contemporary American twist, the atmosphere is soothing, and the food is rich and flavorful.

My mother, sister, and I make Jasmine a regular family gathering spot, where we can get away from the guys and just talk. (I suspect the only place my mother ever really wants to eat is Jasmine, regardless of the time or occasion.)

The menu's specialties are familiar to fans of Thai cuisine, but the flavors here seem more powerfully authentic than many similar places. I think they know by now when I call that my husband wants the garlic beef dish, and I need either the Hung Ray Curry or the ginger pork with mushrooms—all of it with level four heat, by personal request (yeah, we like it spicy). When the day's been especially stressful, Jasmine takeout is almost a necessity.

There are many bigger and more plush Asian-themed restaurants in the city, but this one is special, as anyone who visits will tell you.

Cucumber Salad

(SERVES 2)

Rice powder (instructions below)
Carrot Vinaigrette (recipe below)
2 tablespoons crushed peanuts
1 whole large English cucumber
Kosher salt, to taste
Sugar, to taste
3 teaspoons fresh lime juice
Cilantro, for garnish

To prepare the rice powder: On low heat, sauté about ½ cup of uncooked rice for 10–12 minutes, until lightly browned. Remove from heat, and grind the rice to a fine powder.

To assemble the salad: In a bowl, mix the Carrot Vinaigrette, crushed peanuts, and rice powder. Use vinaigrette lightly so it doesn't pool in bottom of bowl. Add the cucumber and toss thoroughly. Season the salad with salt and sugar to taste and the fresh lime juice. Garnish the plate with chopped cilantro. Serve at once.

Carrot Vinaigrette

1 whole carrot
½ cup rice wine vinegar
1 teaspoon salt
1 teaspoon sugar

Thoroughly rinse the carrot, then shred the carrot completely.

Whisk together the rice wine vinegar, salt, and sugar. Add the shredded carrot and refrigerate overnight.

Just south of Nashville along I-65 lie the towns of Brentwood and Franklin, along with a cluster of smaller communities that make up Williamson County. While independent of the city of Nashville, many of Nashville's largest businesses, including Nissan North America and several major health-care companies, make their homes here, especially in suburban Cool Springs.

The county has a prodigious history and historic sites, including Carnton Plantation (made famous in Robert Hicks's NYT bestseller *The Widow of the South*), the Carter House and the Battle of Franklin site, the Harvey McLemore House, the Lotz House, and a downtown neighborhood of gorgeous historic homes. Quarterly street festivals in downtown Franklin draw enormous crowds. Outside Franklin and Brentwood,

the local farm movement has become a tour de force supplier across the board from farmers' markets to Whole Foods.

Traditionally Williamson County, for all its financial wealth, was notable for its bland chain restaurants. That's changing dramatically: Area chefs like Nick Pellegrino (Mangia Nashville), Jason McConnell and Carl Schultheis (Red Pony, 55South, Cork & Cow), Pat Martin (Martin's BBQ), and others have brought a paradigm shift, building the appetite for good local, chef-driven restaurants. Meanwhile, Nashville entrepreneurs have taken the plunge, opening second locations of popular spots like Porta-Via, Burger Up, Bosco's, Local Taco, and Dan McGuinness Irish Pub in Williamson County.

Small spots like Puckett's Grocery have begun to expand Williamson restaurant empires into Nashville to return the favor by opening locations downtown. Favorite little Brentwood breakfast spot Puffy Muffin opened a second location in Franklin. One of the early, old-school Nashville independent steak houses, Sperry's, opened doors in Cool Springs a few years ago.

Ethnic food has taken hold, too, from longtime resident Thai mainstay Jasmine to outstanding places like Bombay Bistro, Basil Asian Bistro, Wild Ginger, Taste of India, and a host of small sushi joints.

In spite of its reputation for chains and suburban sprawl, a truly interesting and worthwhile culinary culture is taking hold. Add to that growing potential as wine country with Arrington Vineyards, and the beginnings of its own microbrew and distilling community, and there is every reason to be bullish about where Williamson goes from here.

Lockeland Table,
A Community Kitchen and Bar

1520 Woodland Street, East Nashville
(615) 228-4864
LOCKELANDTABLE.COM
Chef/Owner: Hal Holden-Bache
Chef/Co-owner: Cara Graham

While Lockeland Table may be a latecomer on the scene, Chef Hal Holden-Bache is not. I first met him in barbecue god Patrick Martin's kitchen, along with Tyler Brown of Capitol Grille and Tandy Wilson of City House, cooking up a storm for a collection of friends several years ago. Prior to opening his own place, Hal spent time at the late and lamented Nick and Rudy's Steakhouse, then moved on to work at Capitol Grill with Tyler, and then to Eastland Cafe in East Nashville. In 2012 he finally took the plunge and opened up his own place.

Needless to say, Lockeland didn't disappoint—as its nomination as one of the best new restaurants of 2013 from the James Beard Foundation underlines. Not that we had any doubts.

The menu is a mix of the rustic and the refined; consider starters like skillet corn bread and Cox Farm roasted bone marrow (I love bone marrow, and this is superb) to a local cheese plate that lets you pick your own options.

For your main course, choose from a wealth of wood-fired pizzas, or heartier options like a New York strip steak or Carolina mountain trout with maple bourbon glaze. Side dishes range from pommes frites (of course) to grits to braised greens.

Keep your eyes on Hal—anyone who doubts this chef is going places hasn't eaten at his restaurant. And if you can't make it in, here are some real Southern sides to whet your appetite.

97

Southern Corn Bread

(SERVES 6–10, DEPENDING ON THE SIZE OF SERVINGS)

4 cups cornmeal
4 cups all-purpose flour
1 teaspoon salt
¼ cup baking powder
4 eggs
2 cups margarine, melted
8 cups buttermilk
½ cup corn oil

Preheat oven to 375°F.

Mix all the ingredients thoroughly, except the corn oil.

Use the corn oil to grease your baking vessel (cast iron recommended but not required). Bake for 20 minutes or until golden brown.

COLLARD GREENS

(SERVES 6–8)

3 slices smoked bacon
1 yellow onion, diced
4 cloves garlic, chopped
1 shallot
1 cup chicken stock
1 Yazoo dos Perros*
10 dashes Tabasco
¼ cup apple cider vinegar
1 tablespoon granulated sugar
6 bunches collard greens, cleaned and chopped

Bring all the ingredients except the collard greens to a simmer in a thick-bottomed pot at low heat.

Add the collards. Cover and simmer for 2 to 12 hours. Adjust seasonings to taste.

*Note: Yazoo is a local brewing company (see page 154) whose products are increasingly available at specialty beer locations nationally. If you must substitute, use New Belgium Fat Tire or Dos Equis Amber.

THE LOVELESS CAFE

8400 TENNESSEE HIGHWAY 100, ADJACENT TO BELLVUE AND FAIRVIEW
(615) 646-9700
LOVELESSCAFE.COM
CHEF/PITMASTER: GEORGE HARVELL
PASTRY CHEF: ALISA HUNTSMAN

I got my first tastes of the Loveless Cafe over a decade ago, when I was fresh out of grad school and doing regional theater, including performing at local standby Chaffin's Barn Dinner Theatre. The Loveless was just down the road, and often just what the tired actors wanted post-rehearsal. Ah, fried chicken.

By that time the Loveless already had decades of its own history behind it and a series of successful owners, each of which had taken it one step further as a restaurant of note. The most recent ownership has expanded it even further and renovated, but kept the same classic Southern-style feel to the menu that's had people coming back for sixty years or more.

The Loveless has grown to define what people really think Nashville cooking is all about over the years, and in that time they've set themselves up as solid purveyors of good, old-fashioned, home-cooking-style food. Brimming breakfast platters, complete with the restaurant's signature biscuits, make it a favorite breakfast locale.

Supper plates are heaped with standbys: barbecue pork, country-fried steak, traditional homemade meat loaf, fried chicken livers. Pair them with the beans of the day, homemade creamed corn, fried okra, stone-ground grits, or fried green tomatoes—you get the picture. This is serious comfort food.

In 2013 the Loveless got itself a new distinction, as the James Beard Foundation invited them to serve Valentine's Day dinner in the Beard House in New York, re-anointing the cafe as masterful Tennessee traditional cookery.

As you know by now, side dishes are vital necessities in Southern cooking. This carrot pudding is a perfect side if you need to make sure your family members are getting their veggies, even as they devour something rich, creamy, and just faintly sweet.

Homemade desserts have made their place felt in the Loveless's menu, and any visit there had best be made with the intention of following your meal with a piece of pie or a slice of cake. If you don't go that route, you'll regret it for a long time.

The Goo Goo Cluster, for those not familiar, is a native chocolate bar, rich in peanuts, caramel, chocolate, and marshmallow. If you haven't had them yet, order a box at googoo.com.

Carrot Pudding

(SERVES 10)

The Loveless really does side dishes right, and this one is a winner when its sweet lusciousness is paired with serious, savory entrees.

1½ teaspoons salt

4 pounds carrots, peeled and cut in thick slices

¼ pound unsalted butter, melted

½ orange, washed and zested

4 eggs, whipped by hand

1¼ cups sugar

⅓ cup all-purpose flour

1 tablespoon ground cinnamon

1 tablespoon baking powder

Preheat oven to 350°F.

Fill a large pot with water, add salt and boil the carrots until tender. Drain in a colander.

Mash the carrots thoroughly while hot by hand with a potato masher. Stir in the butter. Add the orange zest and squeeze in the orange juice (through a strainer). Stir well.

Add the eggs. Stir.

Fold in the sugar, flour, cinnamon, and baking powder (having previously mixed together well). Stir until all ingredients are well blended.

Pour into a greased casserole dish. Bake until internal temperature reaches 175°F, approximately 40 minutes. Serve hot. Enjoy!

Goo Goo Cluster Pie

(MAKES 1 [9-INCH] PIE, SERVING 8)

3 egg whites
⅔ cup plus 2 tablespoons sugar, divided
¾ cup corn syrup
⅓ cup water
8 ounces semisweet chocolate
½ cup half-and-half
1 teaspoon vanilla extract
2 Goo Goo Clusters, chopped into small pieces
1 (9-inch) graham cracker pie shell
¼ cup chopped roasted unsalted peanuts
1 cup caramel sauce or dulce de leche

Place the egg whites in a large mixing bowl with 2 tablespoons of sugar and mix on low speed. Do not allow it to become frothy; simply mix it enough to dissolve the sugar.

Place the corn syrup and water in a small, heavy-bottomed pot with the remaining ⅔ cup of sugar. Set the pan over medium heat and stir to dissolve the sugar. Using a wet pastry brush, wash the sides of the pot so that no sugar crystals remain, and once the sugar is dissolved, do not stir it. Place a candy thermometer in the pot and cook until the mixture reaches 240°F. While the sugar cooks, you can use the time to make the chocolate ganache glaze.

To make the ganache, place the chocolate and half-and-half into a heatproof metal or glass bowl and set over water that is barely simmering. As it heats, whisk gently to melt the chocolate and make a smooth, glossy glaze.

Next, with a stand mixer on medium speed, whip the egg whites until they are frothy with soft peaks just beginning to form. While the mixer is whipping, carefully pour the hot sugar mixture into the bowl. Take great care to avoid hitting the beaters, or the hot sugar will splatter and can burn. Once all the sugar is added, allow the egg whites to whip fully, until big and fluffy and they resemble marshmallow cream, about 5–8 minutes.

Add the vanilla and continue to whip the marshmallow cream for another minute or two. Remove from mixer and fold in the chopped Goo Goo Cluster pieces.

To assemble the pie, pour 2–3 tablespoons of the chocolate ganache glaze into the bottom of the pie shell and tilt the pan to spread it evenly over the crust. Sprinkle half of the peanuts evenly over the glaze. Once the chocolate glaze is set, transfer the marshmallow Goo Goo filling into the prepared pie shell. Using an icing spreader, decorate the top of the pie with the remaining chocolate ganache glaze. Top it off with the remaining peanuts and chill for at least 1 hour.

To serve, place slices on plates and drizzle each with 2 tablespoons of caramel sauce or dulce de leche.

SUPPER CLUBS & POP-UPS

While larger cities have spent years celebrating the concept of pop-up culture, it's still on the new side for Middle Tennessee, arriving almost in parallel with the sudden burgeoning food truck culture that hit us about 2010.

Pop-ups and supper clubs, like the food trucks, are ideal for those talented chefs who want to refine ideas without yet opening a brick-and-mortar location, and also for food writers and bloggers whose talents lie in directions other than cooking for themselves.

Chefs like Nick Pellegrino (of Mangia Nashville) and Brandon Frohne (Mason's) have absolutely made names for themselves, while gifted food writers like Vivek Surti (viveksepicureanadventures .com) have paired with both chefs and locations like the Nashville Farmers' Market to share their own form of culinary expertise. Most recently in 2013, Sarah Gavigan's Otaku South (facebook .com/OtakuSouth), a pop-up with a focus on traditional Japanese ramen, has taken the city by storm.

Avon Lyons's East Nashville gem, the Goodwife Supper Club, which served groups of sixteen with Sunday-night gourmet dinners, epitomized the best of that scene for us for about nine months in 2011–12. Lyons says she loved writing the menus, creating the descriptions that drew people in, and setting the table—"really the just wonderful, calm pace of it all," she says.

Lyons views our pop-ups as a way for knowledgeable people who've worked in the restaurant community to grow without having to work full-time (she has a young child) and to provide a segue for those shifting careers into the culinary world.

The recent shift of another supper club founder—Lisa Donovan of Buttermilk Road Sunday Suppers, to her current role as pastry chef at Sean Brock's new Husk Nashville—underlines this paradigm perfectly.

From her perspective, Lyons sees these beautiful, transitory things in our food culture leading to a proliferation of smaller, community-focused restaurant spaces—with places like Mas Tacos and Barista Parlor in East Nashville the end result.

Left to right, Vivek Surti, Sarah Gavigan, Tony Galzin, Caroline Galzin, and Lisa Donovan.

MANGIA NASHVILLE

1110 HILLSBORO ROAD, FRANKLIN
(615) 538-7456
FACEBOOK.COM/MANGIANASHVILLE
OWNER/CHEF: NICK PELLEGRINO

We're kind of catching on to the pop-up concept now, but Nick Pellegrino's Mangia Nashville is what brought it to us the first time. Pellegrino is an amazing chef, but he relocated to Nashville for the music business, at which he's been rather successful. The problem was, there was nothing in the city remotely like the New York Italian food he was so used to eating. He began cooking for thrilled family and friends, and eventually hit upon the notion of a weekly pop-up to share, on a small scale, the kind of meals he grew up with.

These days, on most Fridays and Saturdays, Pellegrino and company take over the popular meat-and-three Cool Cafe and turn it into a white tablecloth restaurant. Seating only about sixty to seventy, it's a tough reservation to get, but keep trying till you do.

Over the course of three hours, you'll be served an epic, family-style meal like nothing you've had before, full of pasta and succulent lemon-rosemary chicken, or seasonal baked fishes, or skewers of perfect shrimp.

It's not just the seasonally changing menu—which is marvelous—but the ambiance. You're often seated with complete strangers, who will be friends by the end of the night. Your wine is served in tiny glasses of a kind you haven't seen since *The Godfather*. Mid-meal, the whole crowd gets up and dances, led by Chef Nick beating on a kitchen pot with a wooden spoon, to everything from '50s mambo to '60s Jersey bands like Frankie Valli and the Four Seasons. By the time you leave, you can't believe how much you ate—and that's OK. Mangia is meant to be a night of wild joy, and it pulls it off, every time.

PENNE WITH PORCINI COGNAC CREAM SAUCE

(SERVES 4–6)

"This is one of the richest pasta dishes that we make at Mangia Nashville," says Chef Nick. "The earthy flavor of the mushrooms combined with the cognac, the cream, and the cheeses are almost sinful. I have had customers ask for a straw so they could drink the leftover sauce. Who am I to tell them no?"

2 ounces dried porcini mushrooms

2 cups cognac or brandy, divided

1 cup warm water

6 tablespoons unsalted butter

3 cups heavy cream

1 cup grated Parmesan cheese

1 cup grated Pecorino Romano cheese

1 pound penne pasta, cooked al dente

Salt and freshly ground black pepper to taste

3 tablespoons fresh chopped chives, for garnish

Put the mushrooms, 1 cup of cognac, and warm water into a bowl and let soak until mushrooms are soft, about 20 minutes. Drain the mushrooms, reserving the liquid, and coarsely chop.

In a large skillet or saucepan, melt butter over medium heat. Add mushroom and sauté for 2 minutes. Add remaining cognac to the pan, raise the heat, and let reduce. Once most of the liquid is gone, add the water and cognac that the mushrooms were soaking in. (Be careful not to dump in any grit that might be at the bottom of the bowl from the mushrooms.)

Let this simmer until most of the liquid is reduced. Add heavy cream to pan and gently simmer till reduced by half and it coats the back of a spoon. Stir in both cheeses.

Toss with penne, making sure that sauce covers all the pasta. ("I like to put a teaspoon of butter in at this point. It's already rich—why not drive right off the cliff?" says Chef Nick.)

Season with salt and pepper, transfer to a serving bowl, garnish with fresh chives, and enjoy!

Zeppole

(MAKES ABOUT 35 ZEPPOLE)

"Some of my fondest childhood memories are of my family and I strolling through the San Gennaro Feast with a bag of freshly fried zeppole," Chef Nick reminisces. "I didn't even know who San Gennaro was or what he did, all I cared about was that I was getting zeppole! I knew that if I was to serve them, they could only be presented one way: in a white paper sack filled with confectionary sugar, just like they did at the feast. These have become our signature dessert, and at the end of every night you can see and hear everyone in the place shaking their little white bags. A night at Mangia Nashville is not over till the zeppole have been shaken."

1 quart vegetable oil for frying
1 cup all-purpose flour
2 teaspoons baking powder
Pinch of salt
1½ teaspoons white sugar
2 eggs, beaten
1 cup ricotta cheese
¼ teaspoon vanilla extract
½ cup confectioners' sugar for dusting

Heat oil in a heavy saucepot to 325°F. (Of course, you can use a deep fryer if you have one.)

In a medium saucepan over low heat, combine the flour, baking powder, salt, and sugar. Stir in the eggs, ricotta cheese, and vanilla. Mix till combined. The batter will be sticky. (This can be done several hours ahead of time and fried later. Store in the fridge lightly covered with plastic wrap to prevent a crust from forming.)

Using an ice-cream scoop, drop the zeppole into the oil a few at a time. They will turn over themselves when the first side is done. Fry till the second side is golden brown, about 3 minutes or so. Drain on a cooling rack set over a sheet pan. Transfer warm to paper sacks with confectioners' sugar. Shake and enjoy.

Marché

1000 Main Street, East Nashville
(615) 262-1111
MARCHEARTISANFOODS.COM
Chef/Owner: Margot McCormack

Set right at the apex of the historic Five Points section of East Nashville, Marché is a favorite for just about everyone in the city. The European-style cafe offers up the best in fresh foods daily, from breakfast through dinner, and a fine brunch on Saturday and Sunday (typically packed!). They offer an artisan food market as well, including breads from regional bakers, fresh pastries and cookies to go, locally made Olive & Sinclair chocolates, and a host of similar items residents appreciate.

The atmosphere is open—there's plenty of glass, and the layout allows for a feeling of space. It's one of those restaurants where you're just as comfortable sitting alone and reading while you sip your coffee and relish your meal as you are with a crowd beside you.

I admit I'm usually ordering salads at Marché, because they are always seasonal, innovative, and delicious. But it's typically hard to resist the varying crepes du jour and the ever-changing seasonal entrees—in spring, for example, look for the lamb burger or an egg salad sandwich, while cooler months might bring an open-faced steak sandwich, Moroccan lamb stew, or a pan-seared hanger steak, served with mushrooms and bacon grits.

Of the salad she's provided for the book, McCormack says: "This is on the menu at Marché every spring, and at Margot Cafe often as well. It's one of my favorites."

Salad with Fresh Strawberries, Blue Cheese, Toasted Almonds & White Balsamic Vinaigrette

(MAKES 1 SALAD, WITH EXTRA DRESSING)

1½ teaspoons almonds

½ cup fresh salad greens (Just picked are the best!)

5 fresh strawberries, quartered

1 tablespoon crumbled blue cheese (Your choice, but Marché uses a gorgonzola.)

White Balsamic Vinaigrette (recipe below)

Begin by toasting the almonds lightly in the oven at 350°F for just a few minutes until they are golden brown. Prepare the salad greens by washing and drying thoroughly.

Toss the greens, almonds, strawberries, and blue cheese in an ample bowl. Drizzle the dressing lightly over the greens. (About an ounce per salad is the general rule of thumb—you don't want a soggy salad.) Gently toss together and serve immediately.

White Balsamic Vinaigrette

(MAKES 12 OUNCES)

½ cup white balsamic vinegar*

2 cups vegetable oil

Pinch of salt

1 small shallot, minced

1 teaspoon Dijon mustard

1 teaspoon honey for a little sweetness

Pour the vinegar in a bowl and slowly whisk in the vegetable oil. (Margot prefers vegetable to the heavy olive oil, but you may use that instead if you prefer.) Whisk in salt, shallot, Dijon, and honey.

*Note: You can use any vinegar you like, but the sweetness and color of the white balsamic is the best for fruit preparations.

EAST NASHVILLE

In the early nineteenth century, as Nashville grew up along the Cumberland, wealthier families headed to the east side of the river, building estate homes and genteel farms away from the burgeoning city. In the middle of the century, a host of businesses cropped up, including furniture factories and their requisite saw-mills; the area's commerce flourished. Middle-class neighborhoods expanded, and suburban areas were annexed.

The twentieth century brought a host of disasters: A massive fire in 1916 destroyed more than 500 homes and left thousands homeless, the Cumberland River floods of 1926–27 wrecked property, and a huge tornado in 1933 damaged or destroyed more than 1,600 buildings. The 1940s through '60s saw efforts at "urban renewal," the noisy construction of the interstates, and the fight against school segregation that changed the demographics and popularity of this part of the city.

In the late '70s and '80s, the community began to revive, and especially after the 1998 Nashville tornado, a collection of businesspeople and an artisan community rediscovered the area's appeal. Now, East Nashville booms, with one of the most rapidly growing artisan restaurant and food cultures in town.

The outlying areas are home to plenty of farms, old and new. A weekly farmers' market has developed, and local groceries like the Turnip Truck have emphasized the appeal of fresh, healthy foods to area residents. The trend toward home gardening and canning thrives in East Nashville right now, even as it slowly spreads across the rest of the city.

The past ten to fifteen years have seen the area's restaurant culture flourish, starting with the dynamic Margot McCormack's Margot Cafe and places like Rosepepper Cantina. New restaurants seem to open daily, with restaurateurs like Jason McConnell, well established in other neighborhoods, opening places here. The arrival of Fat Bottom Brewery and Olive & Sinclair Artisan Chocolate, and custom businesses like the Bloomy Rind and Porter Road Butcher, all sourcing their wares to area restaurants, have built the area's reputation. Likewise, folks drive in from Franklin, Green Hills, and West End to hit art galleries, festivals, and boutiques, as well as dine at Silly Goose, Jeni's Splendid Ice Creams, Sweet 16th, Mad Donna's, Pharmacy Burger, and more.

Margot Cafe

1017 Woodland Street, East Nashville
(615) 227-4668
MARGOTCAFE.COM
Chef/Owner: Margot McCormack

Chef Margot McCormack is something of a legend in Nashville. A Culinary Institute of America grad, she is also one of the true "Nashville Originals." Margot helped define local fine dining along with her eponymous restaurant, one of the first to locate in the East Nashville neighborhood in 2001, during its early revival. The building dates to the '30s and was a service station back in the day, set at the heart of Five Points (now just across from McCormack's newer venture, Marché).

Specializing in French country and rustic Italian cuisine, Margot is one of the few area restaurants that emphasize that classical European menu style; it's only recently that the city has really embraced truly French country cookery. Provence and Tuscany shine out from the exceptional daily changing menu that always maintains a solidly established number of appetizers, entrees, and desserts. A strong bar and wine list complements

the menu, with a wide variety of price options and a notable representation of French and Italian options.

The vibe is warm, inviting, and decidedly European in decor and manner. The hidden brick porch is a lovely place to spend a spring evening or a crisp fall one. Simply put, no place else in Nashville is quite Margot.

On a regular menu, you might find an herb-infused olive oil with Parmigiano-Reggiano for dipping bread, house-made potato chips with aioli, a first course of mussels with roasted red pepper sauce and toasts, and entrees including pan-roasted steelhead, grilled lamb chops, and a vegetable pistou.

Of this dish, Margot says, "I love our chicken! This is a very simple preparation highlighting peas, which are one of my favorite things to look forward to each year."

CHICKEN WITH FRESH SPRING PEAS, POTATOES, LEMON & MINT

Per guest to be served:

3 fingerling or small red potatoes
About 1 tablespoon vegetable or olive oil
1 chicken breast
Salt and pepper
⅓ cup fresh peas
Pinch of minced shallot
1 tablespoon butter
1 sprig mint
¼ lemon wedge

Preheat oven to 400°F.

Drizzle potatoes with oil and sprinkle with salt. Roast until they are just soft. Slice the potatoes while still hot, but cool enough to work with. Set aside and keep warm.

In a pan over medium heat, sear the skin side of the chicken until golden brown, then season with a little salt and pepper. Transfer to a 400°F oven to finish cooking. (Use the still-hot oven the potatoes were in.)

While the chicken is cooking, sauté the peas in a warm pan with a pinch of shallot, butter, and fresh mint. Season with salt and pepper.

When the chicken is done to your liking—about 20 minutes cooking time—take out of the oven.

Place 5 or so slices of potatoes on a plate and spoon the peas on top. Place chicken over the vegetables and squeeze with a little lemon. (Margot says she uses their preserved lemon for extra goodness and often enjoys a little crumbled feta over the top as well.)

MARTIN'S BAR-B-QUE JOINT

7238 NOLENSVILLE ROAD, NOLENSVILLE
(615) 776-1856
MARTINSBBQJOINT.COM
CHEF/PITMASTER/OWNER: PATRICK MARTIN

A few years ago, Tennessee native Pat Martin got tired of his landscaping business and decided he wanted to chuck it all and open a barbecue place—the real old-style kind, where whole hogs were roasted all day in the pit. Fortunately for Pat, his wife, Martha, decided this was a good idea, not a pipe dream. Martin found himself a location almost by accident in Nolensville, south of Nashville in Williamson County. When he outgrew that space just a few years later, he built a newer, bigger joint across the street, this one with a real hog pit, so guests can watch as the staff does the cooking—and more importantly, they can smell it.

Things have gone well, and these days Martin is a regular at Big Apple Barbecue, Charleston Food and Wine, and plenty of other national events. He's been featured on *Diners, Drive-Ins and Dives.* And the accolades keep coming.

In spite of that, Pat maintains his commitment to real barbecue, done the old-fashioned way, with the right kinds of sides. When you go, you have to order the pinto beans—just trust me—and make sure you also get an order of barbecue chicken with Alabama white sauce (Martin's is the best, even if it's made in Tennessee).

But the real deal here is hickory-smoked pork. Eat it. Eat lots. It's that good.

Martin provided the instructions for putting together one of his best dishes, the Redneck Taco, but assembly isn't the real thing—you'll need to cook your pork butt in your smoker with hickory. If you can't do that, then go out and buy it pre-smoked from someone who does.

REDNECK TACO

"It's assumed the reader has his/her own versions of pork, slaw, and red sauce," says Martin. I'll let you in on a secret: Your slaw must be light on mayo, heavy on flavor, and Sweet Dixie is a sweet heat–style sauce, so buy accordingly.

(MAKES 1 TACO)

½ cup prepared corn bread mix
1 tablespoon butter, melted
5 ounces pulled pork
4 ounces coleslaw
3 ounces Sweet Dixie sauce, or your favorite sauce

Drop prepared corn bread mix on griddle. With edge of cup, spread it evenly. Allow to cook for about 2 minutes 45 seconds. Carefully flip to other side.

Spread melted butter on top with a brush. Allow to cook for an additional 1 minute 45 seconds. Then plate.

Place pulled pork on top of warm hoecake, then place slaw on top of pulled pork. Pour Sweet Dixie or your favorite sweet-hot sauce on top and serve.

Mas Tacos Por Favor

732 B McFerrin Avenue (brick-and-mortar location and food truck)
(615) 543-6271
facebook.com/mastacos
Chef/Owner: Teresa Mason

We all got used to seeing Teresa Mason's fabulous taco truck hanging out around Imogene + Willie in 12South and downtown, as well as East Nashville, long before there was a brick-and-mortar location we could access readily (that came in 2010). Like most cities in the South, Nashville was slow to touch upon the food truck scene, but Mason was one of our pioneers.

The atmosphere at the Mas Tacos shop is delightful. There's a certain amount of blended Mexican and retro '70s kitsch—with mismatched vintage tables, chairs, and stools; splashes of bright color in art and paint; and heavenly smells emanating from the window to the kitchen—that makes you feel you've still got the truck experience.

If you're there for lunch, chances are you're surrounded by a laughing crowd of people, but the noise level isn't bothersome. It's simply an indication that everyone here is *really* enjoying themselves, and you should, too.

Order your individual tacos from chalkboard menus, grab a Mexican Coke or a Jarritos soda, and you're good to go. Chicken, pork, fish—the tacos of your choice await, paired with fried plantains, black beans or avocados, or perhaps a little chile verde. Everything is delicious. The flavors are balanced and nuanced—it's everything you could want from a taco shop, and would be at home in L.A. as much as Nashville.

This chicken tortilla soup is incredibly popular. I've eaten it more times than I can count, and every single one has been great. Serve as a starter or use it as a main dish with a collection of complementary sides. Count it as spicy comfort food—and the plus side of the spice is that it makes for good summer eating, too.

CHICKEN TORTILLA SOUP

(SERVES 6–8)

1 4-pound chicken

1 onion, quartered

5 cloves garlic, smashed

2 habanero peppers

1 jalapeño pepper (with seeds), halved lengthwise

½ bunch cilantro

3 tablespoons (or more) fresh lime juice

Kosher salt and freshly ground black pepper

For garnish: fresh cilantro, halved cherry tomatoes, avocado wedges, queso fresco, warm soft tortillas, and grilled corn

Bring chicken, onion, garlic, peppers, and about 16 cups water to a boil in a large pot; skim foam from the surface. Reduce heat to medium and simmer, skimming the surface frequently, until chicken is cooked through, about 1 hour.

Transfer chicken from broth. Strain broth into another large pot. Return peppers to broth; discard remaining solids.

Shred chicken meat; discard skin and bones. Transfer chicken meat to a plate and set aside.

Meanwhile, set pot with strained broth over medium heat and add cilantro sprigs. Bring broth to a simmer and cook until reduced to 8 cups, about 1 hour. Discard sprigs.

Stir in 3 tablespoons lime juice. Season with salt, pepper, and more lime juice, if desired. Add chicken to broth; serve in bowls. Pass the garnishes so guests may top as they please.

MASON'S AND MASON BAR

2100 WEST END AVENUE (LOEWS VANDERBILT HOTEL, MIDTOWN/WEST END)
(615) 321-1990
MASONS-NASHVILLE.COM
EXECUTIVE CHEF: BRANDON FROHNE

Mason's and Mason Bar, the newly opened fine-dining establishment in the Loews Vanderbilt Hotel on West End Avenue, made a smart decision when they hired promising young chef Brandon Frohne to open the place for them. Frohne is one of those guys who could have been a statistic, but can honestly say that his drive to be a chef gave him a different future.

Smart, brash, and talented, Frohne appeared on the Nashville restaurant scene a few years ago, barely in his twenties, and became the person we all talked about. He started working in a West End retirement community, created an admirable community garden, and showed off his talents at every possible opportunity. He melded Southern food with modern fusion cuisines, played with molecular gastronomy in a way few people had touched it locally before, and essentially charmed us all the moment we tasted his food. No one could deny his creativity, his talent, or his work ethic.

Mason's menu is about Southern style with a modern focus, something Frohne does extraordinarily well. Add to that a commitment to sourcing locally and seasonally as much as possible, and you have a recipe for something good.

Brandon being Brandon, his contribution was bound to be something you might not normally make at home—but be fearless, this is worth it. The Romesco will likely pair well with other dishes, especially when fresh tomatoes are in season.

Beef Tartare with Pecan Romesco

(SERVES 4)

2 anchovy fillets
2 cloves garlic, chopped
½ cup minced shallots
1 tablespoon drained, chopped capers
2 tablespoons Dijon mustard
¼ cup olive oil
1 teaspoon Worcestershire sauce
1 teaspoon barrel-aged bourbon hot sauce
1 pound beef tenderloin, minced
1/8 teaspoon kosher salt
1 tablespoon cracked black pepper
2 tablespoons Pecan Romesco (recipe on next page)

In a chilled mixing bowl, mash the anchovies, hot sauce, and garlic with a fork to make a paste. Add the shallots and capers and mash them into the paste. Whisk in the mustard.

In a slow, steady stream, add the olive oil, whisking constantly until incorporated. Whisk in the Worcestershire sauce. Add the beef and mix well with a spoon. Season to taste with salt and pepper.

Spoon some tartare on top of the Romesco using a ring mold.

Optional: Garnish with shaved black truffle and crispy potato chips.

Pecan Romesco

(MAKES 2 CUPS)

1 head garlic

1 cup extra virgin olive oil, divided

12 toasted pecans

12 toasted hazelnuts

1 slice stale bread

2 ripe medium-size tomatoes or 1 large tomato

2 large roasted red peppers, well-drained

½ cup sherry vinegar

Kosher salt to taste

Roast garlic by first rubbing off excess dry skin from garlic head. Then place on a baking sheet and drizzle 1 tablespoon of olive oil on top. Roast in the oven for 20 minutes at 300°F or until garlic on inside is roasted and soft.

Place toasted pecans and hazelnuts into a food processor and process until finely ground.

Pour 2 tablespoons of olive oil into a small frying pan and quickly fry bread until both sides are browned. Remove from pan and allow to cool on a plate or paper towel.

Cut tomatoes into eighths and sauté in the same pan, adding oil if needed. Sauté for 4–5 minutes. Remove pan from heat.

Once bread is cooled, tear into pieces and process with the nuts. Add sautéed tomatoes and continue to process. Squeeze roasted garlic from the skins into the processor. Place roasted red peppers into the processor with the other ingredients and process until ingredients are a thick puree.

While processor is running, slowly drizzle in the remaining olive oil and the vinegar. Add salt to taste.

To plate the dish: Mound a circle of 2 tablespoons romesco on a plate, top with 3 ounces tartare mixture that has been molded in a cookie cutter. At the restaurant, Chef Brandon says he adds basil oil to garnish that's optional for an extra burst of herbaceous flavor. You can purchase basil olive oils at most specialty gourmet stores if you wish to add this step.

MERCHANTS RESTAURANT

401 BROADWAY, WEST END
(615) 254-1892
MERCHANTSRESTAURANT.COM
OWNERS: BENJAMIN AND MAX GOLDBERG

In 2010 brothers Ben and Max Goldberg, having already made a name for themselves with the Patterson House, elegant event space Aerial, and a number of other properties through their company Strategic Hospitality LLC, decided to give Merchants a go. The restaurant, once a major fine-dining site in the city on the prominent part of Broadway, had been drifting toward obscurity for years at that point, well after its 1980s and '90s heyday. The brothers purchased the place, in its hundred-year-old building, and decided to revitalize the concept. That turned out to be inspired thinking.

Today's Merchants Restaurant is lighter, warmer, and more welcoming than the old version, and the food is designed to appeal to a vital, younger, more culinary-aware crowd. Perhaps the Goldbergs' most clever choice was essentially creating two restaurants in one: a bright, casual, bistro-esque dining first floor, and a low-lit, more "fine dining" establishment above.

The menus on the two floors vary as well. Downstairs, amid the black-and-white floor tiles, guests nosh on the favorite duck fat tater tots (I haven't had anything else like them that didn't come from a vendor on a French beach), bacon cheeseburgers, blackened tilapia, jambalaya, and the excellent chili recipe provided here. Upstairs, you're more likely to opt for beef tartare, a 14-ounce rib eye, scallops, or roasted pork tenderloin. The Strawberry Salad recipe comes from this side of the restaurant, and makes for a lovely starter before a fish or meat course, especially in spring, when the berries are fresh.

Strawberry Salad

(SERVES 4–6)

A couple of decades ago, Tennessee counted strawberries as one of their major crops. Sumner County, just north of Metro Davidson County, where Nashville proper sits, still grows vast quantities, and Portland, Tennessee, has an annual strawberry festival. It's likewise not surprising that we like our strawberries used any way possible, like this strawberry vinaigrette, served over greens with goat cheese crumbles, which blends the berries' sweetness with the rich bitterness of the balsamic vinegar.

6 ounces mixed greens
2 ounces crumbled goat cheese
1 tablespoon minced red onion
2 tablespoons spicy pecans
¼ cup strawberries
Strawberry Vinaigrette (recipe to right)

Toss the salad ingredients together, and dress with vinaigrette.

Adding chicken or salmon (as shown) makes this tasty salad a heartier choice—Merchants recommends it.

Strawberry Vinaigrette

(MAKES 24 OUNCES)

1 cup strawberry puree
½ cup balsamic vinegar
¼ cup red wine vinegar
6 tablespoons honey
1½ cups vegetable oil
½ cup olive oil

In a blender, combine strawberry puree, vinegars, and honey. Blend at a medium speed for 1 minute. Slowly add the oils to the mixture, and blend until thoroughly combined.

Johnny Cash's "Old Iron Pot" Family-Style Chili

(SERVES 8–10)

Ah, chili—sometimes you just can't go wrong with the classics. You don't have to make this in cast iron, but it won't hurt a bit if you do. This recipe should make chili lovers happy.

For the chili spice blend:

¼ cup paprika
¾ cup Mexene Chili Powder
1 tablespoon cayenne
3 tablespoons cumin
2 tablespoons Chef Paul Prudhomme
   Blackened Redfish Magic
¼ cup sugar
¼ cup salt

For the chili:

2½ pounds ground beef
2 cups minced raw onions
½ cup minced poblano chile peppers
½ cup minced red bell pepper
½ cup tomato paste
3 cups pureed tomatoes
3 cups whole tomatoes
2 cups water
1 Tall Boy (24-ounce) Pabst Blue Ribbon Beer
3 cups cooked red kidney beans
Salt and pepper to taste

In a small bowl, combine the ingredients for the chili spice blend and mix thoroughly.

Brown the ground beef. Add onion and peppers, cooking until translucent. Add ½ cup of the chili spice blend and tomato paste. Cook for 5 minutes.

Add tomatoes, water, and PBR. Bring to a boil and return to a simmer. Let simmer for 1 hour.

Add kidney beans and simmer for 20 minutes. Salt and pepper to taste.

MIDTOWN CAFE

102 19TH AVENUE SOUTH, MIDTOWN
(615) 320-7176
MIDTOWNCAFE.COM
CHEF: BRIAN UHL
OWNERS: RANDY RAYBURN AND BRIAN UHL

Like Cabana and Sunset Grill, Midtown Cafe has evolved from the fine pairing of restaurateur Randy Rayburn and Chef Brian Uhl. Unlike their other ventures, Midtown is set in the heart of—you guessed it—Midtown, and you'll usually find the place packed for weekday lunches and dinners as a result, as it brings in the business clientele from West End Avenue, Vanderbilt, and the nearby Gulch. The menu focuses on great steaks, lamb, veal, and pork—it's meat heavy—and really good seafood. As you might expect from a Rayburn location, there's a remarkable wine list.

This is the place in Nashville where you really do want to start out with the #1 Ahi Tuna Tartare (and, yes, they aim for sustainable seafood), and follow it up with a beef tenderloin filet or a good veal preparation. If there's game on the menu on a given night, with Uhl as chef, take the risk and order it.

Midtown shines in a downtown where you'll find plenty of big chain steak houses, not just for its commitment to sourcing locally where possible and sustainable eating, but because the food truly is outstanding and keeps up with the high Rayburn standards.

I asked Midtown for a starter, and they provided this rich, fabulous smoked salmon option. I don't think you can go wrong trying to impress a dinner party with this one, and the addition of the touch of heat via the Tabasco makes it stand out.

Smoked Salmon Dressing

(SERVES 6)

8 ounces cream cheese

2 ounces anchovies

1 cup chopped garlic

2 cups heavy mayonnaise

2 tablespoons fresh lemon juice

1 tablespoon capers

1½ teaspoons Tabasco

¼ cup fresh dill

3 pounds smoked salmon, roughly chopped

Pull cream cheese from refrigerator and allow to soften.

Meanwhile, place anchovies and garlic in a food processor and process until coarsely chopped. Add mayonnaise, lemon juice, capers, and Tabasco, and process until anchovies and garlic are small flecks.

Add softened cream cheese and pulse until completely incorporated. Add chopped fresh dill and pulse until it is also completely incorporated.

Mix the salmon dressing with the chopped smoked salmon, and serve with toast points or crackers.

MISS DAISY'S AT GRASSLAND MARKET

2176 HILLSBORO ROAD, FRANKLIN
(615) 599-5313
MISSDAISYKING.COM
CHEF: DAISY KING

Miss Daisy King epitomizes the Southern gracious lady, but behind her blazing smile and eloquent words there is the iron-willed talent that started the legendary Miss Daisy's Tea Room as a fearless twenty-something forty years ago, and who remains the grande dame of the Nashville food scene. She remains in constant demand as a caterer, speaker, and consultant, and her books continue to impact new generations of Tennessee cooks. Her Grassland Market–based take-out meals underline her fundamental style and high standard of taste (by more than one definition of that word).

Miss Daisy is a reminder that the best and most quintessential Southern food is based on fresh, seasonal produce made with simplicity. Asked what exemplifies Tennessee cooking, she tells me: "Any Southern heirloom recipe, be it entree, cake, vegetable . . . While we've reached a new level in the South in the past ten or so years, it comes down to a few elements: fresh, simple, pure, but delicious food—true farm-to-table." And, she adds, that's what makes it appeal across the nation these days.

The three recipes that follow are utterly Southern—once upon a time, every Southern homemaker had a cheese wafer/cheese straw recipe she put out for guests. Some of us are lucky enough to have family recipes, but if we don't, this is a fine standard to set now. Hot artichoke dip has had many incarnations at trendy fooderies across the nation since the '50s or '60s, but this is a very basic, simple variation you can make with good Parmesan and know your guests will love it. The black bean salad plays on the popularity of three-bean salads in twentieth century Southern entertaining, but adds a distinctly Southwestern touch. This is one of the dishes she regularly offers for takeout at Grassland Market, and it's irresistible, at least when I'm shopping.

PECAN CHEESE WAFERS

(MAKES ABOUT 75 WAFERS)

8 ounces sharp cheddar cheese
1 cup butter, softened
1½ cups self-rising flour
1 cup finely chopped pecans
⅛ teaspoon cayenne pepper

Grate the cheese, then let it soften with the butter in a bowl. Mix in the remaining ingredients.

Roll dough into logs about 1½ inches in diameter and place them on waxed paper. Chill for several hours.

Slice in thin wafers about ⅛ inch thick. Bake in a 350°F oven for about 8 minutes or until browned.

MISS DAISY'S HOT ARTICHOKE DIP

(SERVES 8 AS AN APPETIZER)

1 (14-ounce) can artichoke hearts, drained
½ cup mayonnaise, or more to taste
½ cup Parmesan cheese
⅛ teaspoon garlic powder, or more to taste
⅛ teaspoon paprika, for garnish

Preheat oven to 350°F.

In a bowl, mash artichokes well. Mix in mayonnaise, Parmesan cheese, and garlic powder.

Pour into a 1-quart ovenware glass dish and bake for 20 minutes or until bubbly.

Sprinkle with with paprika to garnish.

Serve with your favorite crackers, melba toast rounds, or tortilla chips.

Miss Daisy's Black Bean Salad

(SERVES 8, ¾ CUP EACH)

3 cups cooked black beans
1 red bell pepper, chopped
½ green bell pepper, chopped
⅓ medium red onion, chopped
2 green onions, sliced
1 rib celery, finely chopped
3 Italian plum tomatoes, seeded and chopped
1 cup cooked yellow corn
1 tablespoon olive oil
1 tablespoon chopped fresh cilantro
1 tablespoon fresh lime juice
1 tablespoon fresh lemon juice
½ teaspoon hot pepper sauce
½ teaspoon ground cumin
¼ teaspoon salt
¼ teaspoon black pepper

Assemble all ingredients and utensils.

In a large bowl carefully combine the first eight
ingredients. In a separate bowl, whisk together
the remaining ingredients. Pour the dressing over
the salad and toss thoroughly.

THE PATTERSON HOUSE

1711 DIVISION STREET, MIDTOWN
(615) 636-7724
THEPATTERSONNASHVILLE.COM
OWNERS: BENJAMIN AND MAX GOLDBERG

The dynamic Goldberg brothers, Ben and Max, have spent the past several years wonderfully putting their own stamp on Nashville dining. Their revival of old standby Merchants into something that's a well-frequented and innovative eatery made locals take notice, but it was the arrival of the Patterson House Speakeasy that truly set a standard for the city in terms of what we expected from our cocktail culture. (It doesn't hurt that they've opened their hit Catbird Seat upstairs, where the chefs serve up a splendid study in wholly original micro-gastronomy for a thrilled tiny few each night.)

The Patterson House is hidden away on the corner of Division Street in a big, purply-gray house that seems unobtrusive from the outside, but gives way upon entry to a stunning parlor-bar decorated in antiqued mirrors, vintage books, and elegant metallic wallpapers. It keeps that sense of retro 1920s going with its vast bar. Beyond the subtle glamour, the thing that you go for, aside from those little doughnuts that everyone always orders, are the cocktails.

Changing with the season, endlessly innovative, and daring you to step beyond the simple things you've had at every other bar you've ever been to, the Patterson House dares us to take a risk—and we never regret taking it.

DUCK HUNTER

"Sweet Lucy is a whiskey-based orange apricot liqueur—it's sweet and warming with rich fruit notes. Adding an egg yolk provides the drink with a beautiful richness. The allspice lends a nice spice note to the fruitiness, while the lemon adds freshness and acidity. The bitters enhance the orange in the drink," the folks at the Patterson House tell me.

1 egg yolk
2 ounces Prichard's Sweet Lucy Liqueur
¾ ounce fresh lemon juice
¼ ounce St. Elizabeth Allspice Dram
½ ounce simple syrup
9 drops 50/50 Bitters*

Crack the egg and separate the yolk into a shaker tin. Add all the liquid ingredients, including the bitters. Shake all the ingredients once without ice. Add ice and shake again, vigorously. Strain into a small glass with no ice or a coupe glass. Serve.

*Note: 50/50 Bitters are a blend of half Fee's Orange Bitters and half Reagan's Orange Bitters. Buy both Fee's and Reagan's bitters at amazon .com or your favorite specialty store.

Provence Breads & Cafe

1705 21st Avenue South, Hillsboro Village
(615) 386-0363
PROVENCEBREADS.COM
CHEF: CHRIS MASON
BAKER: KEITH BROWN
OWNER: TERRY CARR-HALL
DIRECTOR OF OPERATIONS: KIM TOTZKE

Provence has several locations throughout the city, and they serve the community as our favorite *boulangerie*. Any number of the city's restaurants proudly offer up sandwiches on Provence's wonderful breads. But Provence itself is the kind of place you want to hang out at with friends, drinking deep cups of coffee or tea, eating sandwiches and pastries, and soaking in the atmosphere that is Hillsboro at its best.

Hillsboro Village sits at the confluence of Vanderbilt and Belmont University

neighborhoods, just north of the busy Green Hills suburb. Somehow, though, the energy around it seems calmer, mellower. It's a collection of some of the city's best eateries and charming small boutiques. You can sit and people-watch from Provence's windows almost endlessly, catching sight of big-name stars and ordinary students. (One of the things you must love about Nashville is that stars are rarely harassed—no wonder they want to live here.)

Before I married, I used to sit here with friends constantly. Now it seems I'm always running in and grabbing bread or cookies or handmade salads to go.

Of course, you have to have a bread recipe from Provence, and they've given us a proper baguette. This recipe makes fourteen small loaves—so either plan on freezing some of them or divide it to a smaller proportion for more ready use. It produces a delicious, crusty bread perfect for serving with meals, dipping in oil and herbs, or eating by itself fresh from the oven.

FRENCH BAGUETTES
(MAKES 14 SMALL BAGUETTES)

For the poolish (your starter):

8 ounces bread flour

8 ounces water

Pinch of fresh yeast

For the baguettes:

1 pound poolish

1 pound plus 12 ounces bread flour

1 ounce salt

1 ounce fresh yeast

16 ounces water

Mix the poolish ingredients by hand until wet. Let sit in a covered bowl for 6 hours.

Mix the baguette ingredients by hand until a tight gluten structure forms, about 12 minutes. Let rest for 1 hour.

Divide into 14-ounce pieces and preshape rounds. Shape into baguette forms. Proof on board for 1 hour.

Score tops of loaves. Place in 500°F oven and bake for 30 minutes.

CREAMY TOMATO BASIL SOUP
(SERVES 8–10)

This is one of two takes on tomato soup in this book. You'll find the other in the Grilled Cheeserie entry (see page 90). Each one is delicious; this one relies on heavy cream and white wine, French-style, to give it heft and body, and it pairs really well with some fresh bread for dipping.

2 cups diced onions

¼ cup olive oil

½ cup white wine

¼ cup roasted garlic

12 cups San Marzano–style whole
    stewed tomatoes

Salt to taste

2 cups water

1 cup heavy cream

½ cup roughly chopped fresh basil

Croutons and basil chiffonade, for garnish

Cook onions on medium-high in olive oil until lightly browned. Add wine, garlic, tomatoes, salt, and water and bring to a simmer. Turn heat down to low and let simmer gently for 45 minutes to 1 hour.

Add cream and basil and cook for 15 minutes.

Remove from heat and puree in a food processor for 3–5 minutes until smooth and fully blended.

Garnish with croutons and basil chiffonade to serve.

ELLIE'S OLD FASHIONED DOUGHNUTS

While I'm big into eating healthy generally, I have to admit a weakness for Ellie's Old Fashioned Doughnuts—they might seriously be the best ever, and they're all ours. At a time when Nashville still leans on national trends like overly frosted cupcakes, the delicious simplicity of Ellie's Old Fashioned Doughnuts refreshingly changes the sweet paradigm.

Owner/baker Danny Tassone comes from an upstate New York family with decades of experience in the high-quality grocery, farming, and food business. He made his first true career in the automotive and motor-sport world, but when he decided it was time to shift gears, as it were, he knew food vending was the way to go. Doughnuts weren't so prevalent in the area, so he decided they were the perfect direction in which to focus his energies.

Tassone began with a doughnut tent at the Franklin Farmers' Market in October 2010, selling hot, fresh doughnuts made of the best ingredients: an original cake doughnut, cinnamon and sugar, pumpkin (sometimes with chocolate frosting; this is the best), a delightful blueberry pancake flavor, and so on. He quickly developed a reputation for quality and consistency—we got hooked, and now his doughnut truck also visits the many Franklin street festivals and other events. Next up will be a refurbished 1948 Trotwood camper for weddings, parties, and social gatherings, as well as public functions.

Seriously—Ellie's Old Fashioned Doughnuts are Nashville's best kept secret. Visit them at facebook.com/pages/Ellies-Old-Fashioned-Doughnuts/172601629437949.

PUCKETT'S RESTAURANT & GROCERY

120 1st Avenue South, Franklin
(615) 794-5527
PUCKETTSGROCERY.COM

4142 Old Hillsboro Road, Leiper's Fork
(615) 794-1308

500 Church Street, Downtown
(615) 770-2772
Owners: Andy and Jan Marshall

Andy and Jan Marshall's Puckett's Grocery without a doubt qualifies as a local landmark in Leiper's Fork, perhaps even an icon, as you add together its multiple locations (including the new Puckett's Boathouse just at the outskirts of downtown Franklin, a location in southern Williamson County in Columbia, and the popular alternative food truck, Puckett's Trolley). In the beginning it was about good food and good music, and it still is today, whichever of their restaurants you choose to patronize. A quick perusal of the website will tell you who is playing at which locale and when.

Everyone across the city knows Puckett's, and the downtown Nashville location at Fifth and Church Streets, right next to several of the city's best art galleries, has raised the bar for the restaurant even more.

My most recent visit to Puckett's Franklin location, in the process of writing this book, involved my entire family, including my parents, my visiting aunt and uncle from Virginia, my uncle's sister, and my own sister and her two boys, ages one and five. Needless to say, we were a boisterous table, but it was the perfect place to relax over a long breakfast and have a great visit. Puckett's is a family place—you can bring the kids here and know they'll eat, and there's something for everyone on the menu.

Of course, in the evening when a band is playing, it's the kind of place you can bring a significant other or group of friends, and the atmosphere will be just as appropriate. The menu focuses on good, hearty food, whether you're coming in for eggs, bacon, and French toast at breakfast; a good sandwich for lunch; or a serious dinner that involves a Black Angus rib eye, chicken-fried steak, or the famous cherry-smoked baby back ribs.

PUCKETT'S CHICKEN SALAD

(SERVES 6–8)

Chicken salad is a thing here in the South, and Puckett's version is as traditional as they come, with pecans and fruit. You can feel equally good serving this one on a bed of lettuce to "ladies who lunch" or on some thick slabs of homemade bread to the guys who've been out working all day.

2 pounds chicken breast
1 cup grapes, cut in half
¼ cup pecan pieces
¼ cup diced celery
1 tablespoon sugar
1 teaspoon salt
1 teaspoon white pepper
1 teaspoon thyme
1 cup mayonnaise

Boil chicken breast until done (165°F). Shred the chicken and allow to cool.

Combine the chicken and the remaining ingredients in a mixing bowl. Mix thoroughly and allow to cool.

PUCKETT'S KING'S FRENCH TOAST

(SERVES 4)

When they say it's "King's" French toast, you get they mean Elvis, right? The Memphis-born rock-and-roller did plenty of recording here in town, back in the day, at RCA Studio B downtown. Those days are long gone, but we like to remember the great Mr. Presley by serving meals he would have loved—and we know he loved him some peanut butter and banana sandwiches. Puckett's tribute to that love is this wholly delicious French toast sandwich, perfect for brunch or breakfast. Don't even think about a calorie count.

4 eggs
1 cup heavy cream
1 teaspoon cinnamon
½ teaspoon nutmeg
½ cup peanut butter
8 slices sourdough or egg bread/challah
4 bananas
¼ cup butter
Powdered sugar, to sprinkle

Beat eggs in a mixing bowl. Whisk in heavy cream, cinnamon, and nutmeg.

Spread peanut butter across bread. Cut bananas in half and again lengthwise. Place bananas across 4 of the slices of bread, then top with the rest of the bread to make 4 sandwiches.

Dip entire sandwich into egg and heavy cream mixture.

Butter a griddle pan or skillet on medium heat. Place sandwich onto the buttered surface. Once the sandwich begins to crisp, flip. Brown both sides to desired crispness.

Cut sandwich in half and sprinkle with powdered sugar.

Red Pony

408 Main Street, Franklin
(615) 595-7669
REDPONYRESTAURANT.COM
Executive Chef/Owner: Jason McConnell
Chef: Carl Schultheis

Set in a century-old building off Franklin's downtown square, Red Pony has been the supreme monarch of fine dining in Franklin since Jason McConnell opened it in 2006. Williamson County in general, and Franklin in particular, has been a legendary chain restaurant haven, and McConnell's arrival on the scene did a great deal to help end that reality.

With its aged wood and brick, and soft red, gold, and brown color scheme, the whole restaurant is washed in warmth. From the moment you enter, no matter what it's like outside, the atmosphere soothes you, and it's easy to enjoy your meal, whether you're sitting at the bar watching ESPN or dining with a big group of friends.

I admit spending plenty of time at the bars (there's one upstairs, too), but I've also spent evenings here with friends, gathered around a larger table that still feels intimate. Chef Carl Schultheis pulls off plenty of impressive menu items himself—he and McConnell work brilliantly together.

Sitting at the bar, order from the starter menu—the tempura sushi roll is excellent and generally stays on the menu across seasons, as does the handmade guacamole and a terrific Tennessee tapas plate of local meats and cheeses—and I love the roasted Brussels sprouts as a light meal. When it comes to entrees, if you're partial to Middle Tennessee's take on shrimp and grits, Red Pony does a fine job, and the beef tenderloin is always delicious. For dessert, the pot de crème or the crème brûlée deserves serious consideration. And, of course, nightly specials increase the wonderful options.

Braised Pork Shanks with Red Wine Jus

(SERVES 8)

8 pork shanks (around 1 pound each, on bone)

Salt and pepper to taste

½ cup flour

¼ cup olive oil

2 yellow onions, small diced

2 carrots, peeled and small diced

3 ribs celery, small diced

3 tablespoons chopped garlic

¼ cup tomato paste

1 bottle full-flavored red wine (whatever you like that is inexpensive)

2 sprigs fresh rosemary

2 sprigs fresh thyme

2 bay leaves

Water to cover shanks (meat only) in deep-sided casserole or dish of choice

Salt and black pepper to taste

2 tablespoons chopped Italian parsley, for garnish

Season the shanks generously with the salt and pepper, then dust with flour. Heat a large heavy bottom pan on the stovetop with the olive oil and brown shanks on all sides, working in batches if necessary.

Remove shanks. Add vegetables and sauté until golden brown. Then add the tomato paste and quickly stir into the vegetables. While continuing to stir, cook the tomato paste for about 5 minutes.

Deglaze pan with red wine, and add the herbs and bay leaves. Arrange shanks in your baking dish of choice, add the vegetable mixture and cover the meat with water. Cover the dish with a lid or foil. Place in 350°F oven for approximately 1½–2 hours, or until a skewer slides in and out of meat with ease.

Remove liquid from the dish and reduce on stove top to desired consistency. Season with additional salt and pepper if necessary, to taste.

Garnish with vegetables and reduced red wine jus, and finish with Italian parsley.

Rumours 12th and Division

1104 Division Street, The Gulch
(615) 432-2740
facebook.com/Rumours12thAndDivision
Chef: Jo Ellen Brown
Owner: Christy Shuff

It's been more than a decade since intrepid art gallery owner Christy Shuff (pictured) saw the need for a wine bar in Nashville and created the first version of Rumours. And true to form, as soon as she built it, we came—and we drank deep, enjoyed excellent food, and learned a lot about wine. It became the sort of place we all wanted to just spend time in. For Shuff, regular customers became almost family.

In 2012 tragedy struck, as the charming but nearly outgrown old house that was

Rumours' home was demolished to make way for newer, flashier mercantile space. Shuff did everything right, opting to reopen a few miles away in The Gulch a year later, after much planning and a build-out.

Rumours now rests at the far corner of the ICON building, a stone's throw from the Yazoo Taproom, hidden from the most trafficked bits of The Gulch. She kept Chef Jo Ellen Brown, paying her through the construction phase to ensure the menu's continued continuity. Shuff also kept much of the vibrant art and had the walls repainted in the same splendid deep midnight blue, burgundy, and eggplant purple that old patrons loved so well.

Though famed for wine, the addition of cocktails at this location really broadened the masculine visitorship. The spirits are all boutique, with plenty of familiar Nashville brands. Local beers on tap don't much hurt either. The menu surprises with the return of Rumours' best comfort foods, like the delicious mussel bowls. The tastes and small plates can make a meal on their own, especially with options like the Benton's Bacon Deviled Eggs, the Irish Stout Mac & Cheese, and these terrific Char Siu Meatballs.

No. 1104

Rumours has built its reputation as a wine bar, and there are few that compare in the Nashville area. However, with the opening in 2013 of Rumours 12th and Division, one thing that excited the public was an expanded bar and the promise of artisan cocktails. They're a draw to the guys who don't necessarily favor wine the way their girlfriends or wives do, but they also generally appeal to women—there's no magic focus group, beyond a sophisticated and thoughtful palate. True to form, these are no ordinary cocktails, and bartender Caleb Kimbley, who created this recipe using Tennessee favorite Prichard's, takes his job as mixologist seriously—and we make a regular beeline to Rumours.

1¼ ounces Prichard's Double Barrel Bourbon
½ ounce Cynar
½ ounce Bitter Truth
½ ounce Averna
2 dashes Free Brothers Chocolate Bitters
Orange peel, for garnish

Stir, and pour over ice. Garnish with an orange peel, lightly singed with a baker's torch, if you like.

CHAR SIU MEATBALLS

(MAKES 2 DOZEN MEATBALLS)

For the meatballs:

2 pounds ground pork

1 egg

2 tablespoons minced garlic

2 tablespoons minced ginger

1 tablespoon Chinese Five Spice

2 tablespoons chopped cilantro

1 tablespoon salt

½ cup mayonnaise

½ cup bread crumbs

For the Char Sui Barbecue Sauce:

2 tablespoons soy sauce

3 tablespoons honey

1 clove garlic, minced

1 tablespoon minced ginger

½ teaspoon Chinese Five Spice

½ cup water or chicken stock

1–2 drops of red food coloring, optional

1 tablespoon cornstarch and 2 tablespoons water,
    mixed and set aside

Cilantro, for garnish

Preheat oven to 350°F.

Mix all the meatball ingredients by hand and form into 1-inch balls. Bake for 23 minutes.

Meanwhile, prepare the Char Sui Barbecue Sauce. Heat all the ingredients (except the cornstarch mixture) up in a saucepan on medium heat. Cook 5 minutes. Add the cornstarch slurry to the saucepan. The sauce will thicken pretty fast. If it gets too thick, add a little more water.

When the meatballs are done, toss them in the Char Sui Barbecue Sauce and garnish with cilantro.

Not many years ago, the notion of Nashville native spirits and microbeers would have elicited a look of confusion on the faces of city residents. In less than a decade, that's all changed.

Part of that is due to changes in Tennessee law made under former governor Phil Bredesen in 2009, which now allow for microdistilleries within Tennessee city limits, with voter approval.

Franklin's Mike Williams, the mastermind behind **Collier & McKeel Whiskey,** had a lot to do with lobbying for that law change. Now Williams produces his whiskey up at the **Speakeasy Spirits** campus on 44th Avenue North, in the company of Jeff and Jenny Pennington's Whisper Creek Tennessee Sipping Cream.

Along with him for the ride were Darek Bell and Andrew Webber of **Corsair Artisan Distilleries,** who started out making their spirits in Bowling Green, just across the Kentucky state line, while the state legislature fought it out. (Now only their bourbon is made there; whiskey, gin, vanilla vodka, moonshine, and spiced rum all come from their distillery at Marathon Motor Works.)

If we've gone spirit mad, we've developed an even greater beer culture. **Yazoo Brewery** products are now distributed all over the country, and a good bottle of Pale Ale or Dos Perros can be had by nearly anyone. The all-girl team at nearby **Jackalope Brewery** in The Gulch is producing some very fine beers as well. Micro-chain **Bosco's** had the first female brewmaster in town in the superbly gifted Karen Lassiter (women have beer power in Nashville) making some excellent stuff, and **Blackstone Brewery,** like Bosco's, is an eatery that's made a big name as a brewery now.

East Nashville's Fat Bottom Brewery is taking off fast—that's a great neighborhood for beer—and exciting new places are coming along in Williamson and Rutherford Counties nearby. Murfreesboro's **Mayday Brewery** is deservedly gaining fans. Good local microbrewed beer is dominating even our chain restaurants these days—it's a real win.

SAFFIRE

230 FRANKLIN ROAD, FRANKLIN
(615) 599-4995
SAFFIRERESTAURANT.COM
EXECUTIVE CHEF: VINNY TARDO

Franklin's Saffire restaurant is part of the larger TomKats, Inc.—the parent organization of a number of great eateries in the city and a training ground for TomKats Catering, which provides food on movie sets, backstage at events, and more. Chef Vinny Tardo has been at Saffire for a while now, and his menu never fails to please. I asked for the Chicken Fried Chicken recipe specifically—it's *out of this world*—and was thrilled when they chose to oblige. It takes a bit of time to cook, but it's worth it.

Saffire is set in the Factory at Franklin, a repurposed—you guessed it—factory just outside the historic downtown, home to a diverse collection of boutiques, a small theater company, a wonderful event venue, and other businesses. Spend the afternoon, then make your way to Saffire for dinner and drinks.

With a collection of gorgeously mismatched vintage tables and chairs, a long, broad bar, lots of sapphire blue glass, and the old factory's original glass windows, the place is visually romantic—and it's got plenty of hearty food to bring in big appetites.

While there, make sure you order one of the signature cocktails. The Cucumber Gimlet is always a favorite. Definitely order some fried avocado to start. Then if you don't want the Chicken Fried Chicken, try a peach-glazed pork chop, the center cut New York strip, or perhaps the prime rib. The turnip greens always seem to satisfy. For dessert, try a little Hatcher Dairy Buttermilk Pie.

Mac & Cheese

(SERVES 6–8)

This old-school bit of deliciousness pairs beautifully with the Chicken Fried Chicken, and it also stands on its own just fine. In Nashville you can expect to find homemade variations on the old macaroni and cheese standby listed on "vegetable" plates and as sides nearly everywhere. Saffire offers a meal of four of your choice of sides on their regular menu (you also want the turnip greens and the green beans, and maybe some fries).

This particular variation is made with white cheddar and just a bit of white pepper—it's truly old-fashioned, but that's no bad thing. Rich, creamy, and delicious, you can feed this to your kids—or save it as a very adult treat for a dinner party.

3 tablespoons all-purpose flour

3 tablespoons butter, melted

2 cups milk

½ teaspoon salt

Pinch of white pepper

Pinch of granulated garlic

½ cup shredded white cheddar

4 cups penne pasta, cooked and drained

In a medium saucepan over medium heat, combine flour and butter. Mix together milk, salt, white pepper, and granulated garlic and add to flour/butter mixture.

Cook for about 2 minutes, until sauce begins to thicken. Whisk in shredded cheddar slowly, until it is fully incorporated.

Mix the penne with the sauce carefully, ensuring it is completely coated, and serve. If serving with chicken fried chicken, in the restaurant it is frequently plated with the chicken set on top of the mac and cheese.

Chicken Fried Chicken

(SERVES 4)

For the chicken:

4 boneless, skinless chicken breasts
2 cups buttermilk
2 ounces hot sauce (Louisiana Hot Sauce preferred)

For the breading and to fry chicken:

3 cups all-purpose flour
3 cups panko bread crumbs
½ cup Bad Byron's Butt Rub or other barbecue
    seasoning
Shortening to fry chicken

For the gravy:

½ cup flour
¼ cup butter, melted
2 shallots, minced
2 cloves garlic, minced
1 cup minced country ham
1 quart heavy cream
1 cup chicken stock
1 teaspoon cracked black pepper

To prepare the chicken: Cover a cutting board with plastic wrap and lay out the skinless chicken breasts. Cover the top with another layer of plastic wrap. Lightly pound chicken breasts to uniform thickness.

Place in a 2-inch-deep plastic container or casserole dish and cover with buttermilk and Louisiana Hot Sauce.

Place in refrigerator for at least 20 minutes. If you wish to make things in advance, it can be left overnight, but should not be left in the mixture longer than one day.

To bread and fry chicken: Combine flour, panko, and butt rub. Incorporate well.

Heat enough shortening in a cast-iron skillet or Dutch oven over low heat to come about ½ inch up the side. Once shortening liquefies, raise heat to 325°F. Do not exceed 350°F.

Take chicken out of marinade and coat well with breading. Shake off excess and place carefully into oil. Cook for about 3 minutes per side, until outside is golden brown and internal temperature has reached 180°F.

Do not overload pan. Cook 1 to 2 breasts at a time, depending on size of pan.

To make the gravy: In a small bowl, combine flour and melted butter and mix well to make blonde roux. Reserve.

In a medium saucepan over medium heat, sweat shallots and garlic until translucent. Add minced country ham and cook 1 minute. Before garlic browns, add cream and chicken stock. Add black pepper and bring to a boil. Once boiling, add roux and whisk together well. Set aside.

Plate components (pairs nicely with Saffire's Mac & Cheese on previous page) and enjoy.

SILLY GOOSE

1888 EASTLAND AVENUE, EAST NASHVILLE
(615) 915-0757
SILLYGOOSENASHVILLE.COM
CHEF: RODERICK BAILEY

One of my favorite regular stops in East Nashville is the Silly Goose, for its innovative menu and its warm, eclectic style. Keeping with the growing emphasis in the city on fresh and local, they make use of a plethora of local suppliers, including Silke's Old World Breads, Kenny's Farmhouse Cheese, Green Door Gourmet, TruBee Honey, and Noble Springs Dairy, among others. Nashville loves our burgeoning local artisan food movement, and it seems regularly on display at Silly Goose. Set back on Eastland Avenue, it is the epitome of the neighborhood restaurant that seems to be thriving across all regions of the city.

I almost always order one of the couscous dishes when I go in for lunch, usually paired with their herbal lemonade. There are always at least four options on the menu, with flavors ranging from the true Mediterranean of the Sicilian, with capicola, roasted red pepper, almonds, basil, kalamata olives, blue Gouda, and a balsamic reduction, to the south-of-the-border spiciness of red chili couscous, grilled chicken, poblano peppers, cilantro, goat cheese, mango, and lime juice that make up the Mexico City.

I'm thrilled that this is the recipe they were kind enough to provide, however. I love bold, South Asian curry flavors, and this is one of my favorite lunches—it really underlines the kind of creative and original cookery Silly Goose is known for.

PULLED PORK WITH CARAWAY SLAW & HOMEMADE DIJON MUSTARD

(YIELD: 2 QUARTS)

This recipe can probably feed a picnic of twenty, but the extra dressing and Dijon (recipe on page 166) can be saved for other uses, and the amount of pork can be reduced to suit your needs.

PULLED PORK

4 quarts water
¼ cup cloves
¼ cup allspice
3 teaspoons peppercorns
3 teaspoons mustard seeds
3 teaspoons ginger
4 cinnamon sticks
2 cups salt
Skinned, boned pork shoulder, up to 6 pounds,
    cut into chunks (Boston butt is also acceptable.)

Mix all ingredients except pork in a large pot and bring the brine to a boil, cool, then pour over the pork.

Soak the shoulder in brine for 8 days, turning daily.

On the 8th day, remove the pork from the brining container and put into a deep pan. Bake the pork at 300°F, covered, for 1 hour, then check internal temperature with a digital thermometer every 20 minutes. The small pieces will be done first.

Remove and let cool completely in the juice.

When cool, shred the pork using a good fork. The meat should break apart easily.

CARAWAY SLAW

½ cup caraway seeds
1 pint sour cream
⅓ cup apple cider vinegar
1 tablespoon honey
1 teaspoon mixed salt and pepper
2 quarts cabbage, thinly sliced

Toast the caraway seeds in a pan, then puree half of the seeds in a spice grinder. Mix the remaining ingredients, including the remaining caraway seeds but not the cabbage, in a bowl with a whisk. Store (labeled and dated) if you don't use all of it to make your slaw.

Add the caraway dressing to your slaw, as needed, to taste. Some will prefer a more heavily sauced version, some a lighter touch, since caraway is a distinct flavor. You may use a prepackaged cabbage slaw, or cut your own cabbage into the size you prefer.

HOMEMADE DIJON MUSTARD

(MAKES 2 CUPS)

⅔ cup water, plus additional water as needed

1 cup dry mustard

2 cups cider vinegar

½ cup finely chopped onion, scallion, or your
favorite type of onion

1 head garlic

2 bay leaves

2 tablespoons peppercorns

8 juniper berries

2 teaspoons salt

2 tablespoons sugar

Combine ⅔ cup water and mustard powder.
Set aside.

Combine the remaining ingredients in a
saucepan. Heat on the stove and reduce by
two-thirds, then strain.

Add the mustard powder–water mixture to the
reduced ingredients, and return to the stove for
15 minutes. Add more water as needed until the
total amount of Dijon equals 2 cups.

To assemble the sandwiches: Use all the
components in desired quantities to make
sandwiches with fresh multigrain bread. Sloco
makes their bread at the store, but you can
choose your favorite as well!

THE SOUTHERN STEAK & OYSTER

150 3RD AVENUE SOUTH, DOWNTOWN/SOBRO
(615) 724-1762
THESOUTHERNNASHVILLE.COM
OWNER: TOMKATS, INC.

One of the newer downtown restaurants to come along, the Southern Steak & Oyster first made waves because it provided a truly good place to have a serious breakfast meeting over good food downtown. They manage far more than an excellent breakfast, fortunately, including lunch, dinner, Sunday brunch, and up until midnight on the weekend, if you happen to wander over from the grand, glorious Schermerhorn Symphony Center next door after a concert. That it happens to sit at the top of the Pinnacle Building, providing incredible city views as you dine, doesn't hurt either.

The Southern is part of the TomKats family, meaning they put a quarter century of highly successful catering and restaurant business knowledge behind this venture. They've put a lot of thought into what makes this place work—and while the focus, as the name suggests, is really steak and oysters (via a state-of-the-art, shuck-to-order oyster bar), there's plenty more on the menu to grab your attention.

The Southern strives to be many things—it's got both casual and fine-dining space and a comfortable bar where you can sit back and be yourself. What you find yourself appreciating is that it can successfully be many things at once and still define itself effectively, via a solid menu that emphasizes Southern foods with a little bit of twist—think of it as a branch of New American cuisine.

I really love this as a breakfast spot, I have to admit, but there's plenty to be said for drinks and oysters late on a summer afternoon, as my friend Dara Carson and I can attest.

BBQ Shrimp

(SERVES 2 AS AN APPETIZER)

The Southern has seafood clearly in its sights—that's obvious. This is a marvelous alternative to a traditional shrimp cocktail and a terrific way to start off a meal.

3 tablespoons diced onion

1 teaspoon chopped garlic

1 tablespoon olive oil for cooking

5 large head-on shrimp

Salt and pepper to taste

2 tablespoons white wine

¼ cup BBQ Butter (recipe at right)

Chopped chives and grilled slices of French bread
    for garnish

Sauté onions and garlic in olive oil until soft, approximately 1 minute. Add shrimp and cook for another 3 minutes. Season with salt and pepper. Deglaze with white wine and reduce by half.

Add ¼ cup BBQ Butter and cook until butter is melted and shrimp are cooked.

Place shrimp and all of the pan's contents in a shallow bowl and garnish with chopped chives and grilled French bread.

BBQ Butter

(YIELD: ABOUT ½ CUP)

1 stick (½ cup) unsalted butter, room temperature

2¼ teaspoons lemon juice

¾ tablespoon minced shallot

½ tablespoon Cajun seasoning

½ tablespoon paprika

¾ teaspoon minced garlic

¾ tablespoon chopped parsley

¾ teaspoon Worcestershire sauce

¾ teaspoon salt

Mix butter in an electric mixer with a paddle attachment until smooth. Add all the remaining ingredients and mix until incorporated, scraping sides of bowl with a spatula to ensure seasoning is distributed evenly.

My Way (Pasta)

(SERVES 1)

Fans of spaghetti carbonara will love this tomato-free variation on eggs and pasta. With bacon lardons and goat cheese, you can easily serve this as a breakfast or brunch dish, but that doesn't preclude using it at dinner. I'm a big fan of pine nuts and cook with them every chance I get—they add a lovely nutty flavor to this dish that really seems to complete it.

2 tablespoons butter

1 teaspoon chopped garlic

2 ounces bacon lardons, cooked

5 ounces linguine, cooked

Salt and pepper, to taste

2 farm-fresh eggs

3 ounces goat cheese

2 tablespoons toasted pine nuts

1 tablespoon scallions, plus extra for garnish

Melt butter over medium heat and cook until milk solids begin to brown. Quickly add garlic and bacon lardons to pan and cook for 30 seconds.

Add linguine and season with salt and pepper. Continue to cook until hot.

Add 1 whole egg. Break and scramble throughout the pasta until egg is cooked.

Add goat cheese, pine nuts, and scallions. When cheese melts, plate the pasta.

Cook the remaining egg sunny-side up and place on top of the pasta. Garnish with chopped scallions.

Sunset Grill

2001 Belcourt Avenue, Hillsboro Village
(615) 386-3663
sunsetgrill.com
Chef: Chris Cunningham
Sous Chef: Daniel Glavan
Owner: Randy Rayburn

In 1990 Randy Rayburn, trained at the Culinary Institute in Hyde Park and already possessed of a good history in the Nashville restaurant business, got tired of working for someone else. He "threw every chip on the table": He quit his job, sold his house, and put everything he had down on a 2,200-square-foot former bicycle shop. Now, twenty-three years and seven expansions later, Sunset Grill remains one of the area's most beloved restaurants, anchoring the popular Hillsboro Village.

The menu has changed to match the times, though it's always been ahead of the trends—chef driven, making use of the local farm sources where possible, and forward-thinking in its pursuit of excellent wines from day one. The delicious, spicy Voodoo Pasta that Rayburn created is still on the menu, but the rest has shifted to meet the present needs of myriad customers across ages and demographics.

"I believe that food is edible art," says the genial Rayburn. "Our menu evolves with the times and the audience."

It's the rare place where the staff and the atmosphere stay consistent. "We're about creating a culture with our staff and team members," says Rayburn. "We're passionate about food and wine as part of our lives. This is *what we do*."

A diverse menu replete with hearty entrees like grilled Scottish salmon, Coca-Cola beef short ribs, or braised lamb shank; original, creative salads (the Beets & Heat Salad below is a favorite, and the Caesar is excellent); and thoughtful daily specials keeps it interesting.

A casual lunch or dinner at Sunset may reveal a celeb or political figure across the room—or your best friends—but no touch of pretense or haughtiness. The crowds perpetually come for the original menu, the diverse, lengthy wine list, and the outstanding service, not to see and be seen. That's just the kind of place Rayburn aims to keep for us.

Beets & Heat Salad

(SERVES 4–6)

2 pounds golden beets, diced
2 tablespoons olive oil, or more to taste
Salt to taste
1 pound fresh arugula
1 head fennel, julienned

2 oranges, segmented
Tabasco Honey Vinaigrette (recipe at right)
½ pound goat cheese/chèvre
½ pound candied pecans (recipe at right)

Preheat oven to 350°F.

Toss the diced beets in extra-virgin olive oil and salt to taste. Roast for about 45 minutes, until tender. Allow beets to cool to room temperature before the next step.

Thoroughly mix beets, arugula, fennel, and oranges with vinaigrette. When ready to serve, garnish with goat cheese and candied pecans.

CANDIED PECANS

½ pound whole pecans
2 egg whites
½ teaspoon salt
¼ cup sugar
½ teaspoon ground cumin
½ teaspoon cayenne

Preheat oven to 325°F.

Mix all the ingredients. Strain off the excess egg whites, then place the pecans on a nonstick silicon pad.

Roast for 12–15 minutes, then cool before using to garnish your salad.

TABASCO HONEY VINAIGRETTE

¼ cup Tabasco
½ cup clover honey (or honey to your liking)
½ cup vegetable oil

Mix all the ingredients together until thoroughly combined.

SHRIMP & GRITS WITH PICKLED OKRA

(SERVES 6)

Shrimp and grits in the South comes in many forms. Once upon a time it was a Low Country specialty you only saw in Charleston or Savannah, but that moment has passed. Now most cities in the South have their own takes on the dish, and its popularity is spreading well beyond the borders of the traditional South, as residents of the North and the Midwest discover the humble grit.

This one adds fun with the pickled okra—another traditional Southern food finally getting some play outside the bounds of the Mason-Dixon.

For the grits:

½ quart chicken stock
½ quart heavy cream
2 teaspoons salt
Pinch of pepper
1 cup grits
¼ pound white cheddar

For the Tabasco butter:

1 pound butter, softened
¼ cup Tabasco
1 teaspoon honey
Pinch of salt

For the shrimp:

36 shrimp
1½ cups sliced red bell peppers
1½ cups sliced onions of your choice
Olive or canola oil to sauté

To make the grits: Heat all the ingredients except the grits and cheese in a pan on the stove. Turn the heat to low, then add the grits.

Stir frequently until soft, about 30 minutes, then add the cheese.

To make the Tabasco butter: Mix all the ingredients together thoroughly, using a mixer.

To prepare the shrimp and assemble the dish: Sauté the shrimp, bell peppers, and onions in oil until the shrimp is halfway cooked. Add the Tabasco butter and continue to cook until shrimp is done. It should be pinkish white and no longer translucent. Serve over the grits, garnished with pickled okra (recipe below).

PICKLED OKRA (YIELD: 16 OUNCES)

2 cups water
2 tablespoons sherry vinegar
2 cups cider vinegar
¼ cup garlic; sliced or whole cloves depending
      on your taste
10 black peppercorns
¼ cup salt
½ cup sugar
1 teaspoon crushed red pepper
2 pounds okra

Bring all the ingredients except the okra to a boil. Thoroughly clean the okra for use and set aside in a separate container. Once the brine boils, pour it over the okra so the vegetables are entirely submerged.

Refrigerate for 24 hours before using. A sealed jar is recommended. And leftovers will keep in the fridge.

JACK DANIEL'S PECAN PIE

(MAKES 1 [9-INCH] PIE, SERVES 8)

Randy Rayburn's Sunset Grill is a perfect place to stop by if you just want to enjoy a dessert with a glass of wine or a cocktail at odd hours (or after dinner, but sometimes you really just want dessert). They have thoughtfully provided the recipe for their toothsome chocolate pecan pie, with a touch of Tennessee added courtesy of a little shot of Jack Daniel's in the mix. Serve it with some vanilla bean ice cream or by itself.

3 eggs

1 cup dark corn syrup

½ cup sugar

2 teaspoons vanilla extract

2 ounces melted butter

¼ cup Jack Daniel's whiskey

1¼ cups pecan pieces

1¼ cups semisweet chocolate chips

1 frozen 9-inch pie shell (thawed, but chilled)

Preheat oven to 325°F.

In a mixing bowl, mix the eggs, corn syrup, sugar, vanilla extract, melted butter, and whiskey and place to the side.

In a separate bowl, mix the pecans and chocolate chips, then put them inside the pie shell. Next, fill the shell with the liquid mixture.

Bake for 35 minutes. Remove from oven and cool before serving.

WILD & LOCAL

Nashvillians love seafood, which is sometimes ironic given Tennessee's lack of a sea coast. We do have a fair amount of freshwater, and with that comes plenty of freshwater fish, but we covet those from saltier sources.

Fortunately, we're blessed with some great suppliers. I recently came across Wild & Local, one of the best of those, via their shop in the Nashville Farmers' Market. It astonished me that I hadn't realized the quiet men in the corner stall of the market house were fishmongers, but it was a fortuitous discovery.

Though most of the day's seafood was destined for restaurants (their clients include most of the establishments in this book, among them Flyte, Red Pony, Table 3, 1808 Grille, Sunset Grill, Saffire, Yellow Porch, Merchants, and City House), passersby can purchase the rest for themselves—which we do.

A newer company (circa 2011) with a bold goal of sustainability, Wild & Local Foods sees their mission as an effort to encourage chefs and home cooks to understand exactly from whence their food came, and how it was caught and raised. They source fish from the fishermen and other meats locally from Tennessee farmers (they also deal in game meats, beef, pork, and poultry).

On my last visit, an ever-changing chalkboard above the shop front listed the food available and the market price. It's not cheap, but the quality is exceptional. On that day I bypassed the Louisiana redfish, the crawfish, and the halibut, but took home fresh diver scallops from Maine and oysters from the Gulf Coast. They were delicious, and for a Nashville home cook, not just a typical dinner.

Wild & Local is at 900 Rosa L. Parks Boulevard, inside the Nashville Farmers' Market; wildandlocal foods.com.

SWAGRUHA

900 ROSA L. PARKS BOULEVARD
(NASHVILLE FARMERS' MARKET),
GERMANTOWN
(615) 736-7001
SWAGRUHAINDIANRESTAURANT.COM
OWNER: SIVA PAVULURI

I've been a big fan of Indian cuisine since I can't remember when, and Nashville's Indian restaurants are excellent. One of my absolute favorites is Swagruha, inside the Nashville Farmers' Market. Owner Siva Pavuluri makes me feel utterly at home every time I go. When I was working from an office downtown, that was once a week—so I got to know her rather well. So well, in fact, she once brought me a gorgeous violet-and-green silk scarf back from a trip to India—which speaks to her generosity as well as her talent in the kitchen.

When you arrive at Swagruha for lunch, there's inevitably a line, with customers of every possible ethnic background, all looking for a very excellent meal.

There's nothing I've tried here that isn't delicious—I could, and have, make a meal out of the samosas—but really, Siva excels with her excellent butter chicken and chicken tikka masala. Fortunately, when you order from her counter, you can try both, and a bit of her equally fabulous vegetable korma, over a bed of fragrant vegetable rice.

For those looking to serve a vegetarian main course (not vegan, since there is yogurt involved), this is a wonderful meal all in itself. Rich and full of spices, it will make your kitchen smell like heaven and your guests very happy.

VEGETABLE KORMA

(SERVES 8–10)

5 medium-size potatoes

1 cup diced carrots

½ cup vegetable oil

½ teaspoon mustard seeds

½ teaspoon cumin seeds

2 cups sliced onions

3 teaspoons salt

1 teaspoon turmeric

1 cup green peas

1 tablespoon chili powder

1 teaspoon ginger garlic paste (available at international grocery stores)

2 medium-size tomatoes, diced

¼ cup grated coconut

2 cups yogurt

1½ teaspoons garam masala powder

1 tablespoon chopped coriander leaves (optional)

Cut potatoes into halves, then boil and peel. Cut the potatoes into ½-inch squares. Boil diced carrots.

Heat oil on medium-high for 2 minutes, then add mustard seeds. When the mustard seeds begin to pop, add cumin seeds. Add onions, salt, and turmeric and sauté until onions are clear. Add potatoes, carrots, and green peas.

Fry on medium heat for approximately 10 minutes. Then add chili powder, ginger garlic paste, and tomatoes and continue to fry on medium heat for an additional 5 minutes.

Add grated coconut, yogurt, and garam masala. Cook on low heat for approximately 10 minutes or until the oil rises to the top. Optionally, garnish with coriander leaves.

Serve with rice, naan, or roti.

TABLE 3 RESTAURANT & MARKET

3821 GREEN HILLS VILLAGE DRIVE, GREEN HILLS
(615) 739-6900
TABLE3NASHVILLE.COM
CHEF: WILL UHLHORN
OWNERS: WENDY BURCH AND ELISE LOEHR

Wendy Burch and Elise Loehr had already proved their mettle with F. Scott's when they took on a challenge: French bistro/brasserie Table 3, complete with an adjacent patisserie—Table 3 Market and Bakery, so customers could not only come in for a good meal, but also take home a few sandwiches, cookies, or the take-out Blue Plate of the Day if they don't have time to linger.

It is perhaps unexpected that French country cuisine has not had a big following in Nashville until now. We've had our proliferation of Italian food, but it's only in the past few

years that we've really come around to appreciate French as we ought. Table 3 brought French culinary sensibilities to the heart of Green Hills—arguably the busiest and most bustling shopping and business district in the city.

This is the place you can go if you want those fried frogs legs, *frisée aux lardons,* or crispy duck confit as starters, to be followed with cassoulet, rabbit fricassee, or coq au vin (I recommend it here). It's true French cookery, the way you want it done, with every aspect properly tended to. Table 3 stands out for the quality of its food, the breadth of its wine list, and an atmosphere reminiscent of true brasserie style.

I am thrilled to have the bouillabaisse recipe below—there's nothing that says true French cookery like it, and Table 3's is a hearty meal that reminds us why we wish we had more trips to the French coastlands planned.

Onion Soup Gratinée

(SERVES 6)

I think if you polled people and asked them to name a single French dish, the vast majority would respond with "French onion soup." I suspect there's a very good reason for that answer—it's flavorful and hearty, and there's absolutely nothing like it when on a cold, rainy day. The depth of this particular recipe allows for a myriad of flavors to balance out the onion, making it smooth and luscious.

1 bay leaf

3 sprigs thyme

2 cloves garlic

¼ cup black peppercorns

2 tablespoons butter

5 yellow onions, julienned or finely sliced

1 teaspoon salt

¾ cup sherry

1 cup brandy

3 cups veal stock

1 quart chicken stock

Salt and pepper to taste

1 baguette or white country bread, toasted
     and cut to fit individual bowls

6 slices Gruyère cheese

Additional items:

Cheesecloth

String

Oven-safe soup bowls

Make a sachet of the bay leaf, thyme, garlic, and black peppercorns by wrapping them in cheesecloth and tying off with string. Put aside.

Melt the butter in a medium-size sauce pot over medium heat. Add onions and salt, stirring frequently for 5 minutes, then reduce heat to low. Continue cooking, stirring as needed, until caramelized, about 30 minutes.

Raise heat to medium-high and add sherry and brandy. Reduce liquid by half.

Add veal stock and chicken stock and bring to a simmer. Add the sachet and simmer with the stock for about 45 minutes. Remove the sachet and season to taste with salt and pepper.

Preheat the broiler to high.

Ladle the soup into individual soup bowls. Float toasted baguette/bread slices, top with Gruyère, and broil until golden brown and bubbling, about 3 minutes.

Tavern

1904 Broadway, Midtown
(615) 320-8580
TAVERNNASHVILLE.COM
Executive Chef: Jay Flatley
Owner: Chris Hyndman

Let me say that of all the M Street properties Chris Hyndman has opened, I unabashedly favor Tavern. Tavern took the best elements of Lime, the restaurant he formerly operated in the same Midtown spot, and the things that worked well over at Whiskey Kitchen, melded them, and then allowed it to take on its own identity. The result is a pleasant respite in the midst of the crazy traffic just off Broadway and Division Street, where you're happy to get away from the workaday world, even if it's for a work meeting. In the evening in mild weather, you sit with the doors rolled up, enjoying the breeze and the bustle of the city.

Jay Flatley is a relative newcomer to the place, but he's done fine things to make the menu his own, and fans of the restaurant look forward to more from him.

Tavern has some of the best salads around. The Tuscan Kale & Parmesan Salad really does convert non-kale-eaters to kale (full disclosure, I eat a lot of kale). And you must appreciate the exquisiteness of A Salad of Little Gems, which showcases red pear, cranberry, and fresh ricotta, all tossed in a toasted almond vinaigrette.

I'm happy, however, that the restaurant has provided a salad many of us food writers really like—the Thai Cobb, which pairs grilled chicken with edamame in a savory Asian fish-sauce vinaigrette.

THAI COBB SALAD

(SERVES 4–6)

2 boneless chicken breasts, cooked (either grilled or poached) and cooled
2 heads Napa cabbage, shredded
½ green papaya, finely julienned
2 large carrots, peeled and finely julienned
1 cucumber, peeled, seeded, and chopped
¾ cup dry-roasted unsalted peanuts, barely crushed
½ cup edamame beans
Fish Sauce Vinaigrette (recipe below)
2 limes, cut into 6 wedges each, for garnish
1 full bunch cilantro, leaves only, for garnish

Chop the cooled chicken into ¼-inch pieces or pull apart with hands.

Combine the chicken and all the other salad ingredients in a large bowl.

Add vinaigrette and combine gently to cover salad. Portion into desired servings and garnish with lime wedges and cilantro.

FISH SAUCE VINAIGRETTE

½ cup fish sauce
⅓ cup water
1½ tablespoons rice wine vinegar
Juice of 1 lime
¾ cup granulated sugar
2 cloves garlic
3 jalapeños, seeded

Combine all the ingredients in a blender and process for 3–5 minutes, until sugar is dissolved. If a tabletop blender is unavailable, a handheld stick blender and a tall container will suffice.

WHISKEY KITCHEN

118 12TH AVENUE SOUTH, THE GULCH
(615) 254-3029
WHISKEYKITCHEN.COM
EXECUTIVE CHEF: TONY PATTON
OWNER: CHRIS HYNDMAN

Entrepreneur Chris Hyndman developed his M Street concept by making use of an entire city block downtown in the old, revitalized railroad gulch. After a local favorite, Radius 10, closed several years ago, he worked to turn that location and its mostly industrial block running along McGavock Street at the corner of 12th Avenue South into a concept collection of remarkably different restaurants. These included trendy Asian-fusion Virago, high-end steak house Kayne Prime, and a private members-only club. Right at the corner of the two streets, he turned a former Mexican restaurant into Whiskey Kitchen—and we loved it.

Boasting a plethora of really enjoyable menu items that play on the notion of Southern comfort foods, including some of the best sweet potato fries and sliders in town, Whiskey Kitchen also boasts a really amazing bar—and a solid tasting list of whiskeys, for those so inclined. The cocktails are plentiful as well, and very creative.

During the day you'll find plenty of folks taking a business lunch here or meeting for drinks after dinner. The outside pergola provides a welcome respite from the bustle of

nearby Broadway. I spent a lot of time sitting here with coworkers in my magazine days, and plenty of late nights after concerts at nearby 12th and Porter with my music and fashion friends as well.

The recipe provided here is another take on the quintessential Tennessee favorite, macaroni and cheese. This is a little on the grown-up side, with a hint of heat to it. Definitely perfect to serve for your friends at a football party or the like and have them begging for more.

CHIPOTLE MAC & CHEESE

(SERVES 4)

8 ounces pasta shells or elbow macaroni
¼ cup unsalted butter
3 tablespoons flour
3 cups half-and-half
2 cups shredded white cheddar
½ cup white or yellow American cheese
1 teaspoon onion powder
1 teaspoon garlic powder
Salt and pepper, to taste
1–3 tablespoons chipotle peppers in adobo,
    minced or pureed
½ cup buttered bread crumbs. optional

Cook pasta of choice to al dente.

Melt butter over medium heat. Add flour and stir to make a roux.

Slowly add half-and-half to pot with roux, stirring until smooth. Continue to stir until sauce begins to thicken.

Add cheeses a little at a time, stirring constantly until smooth, then add spices, salt, pepper, and chipotle peppers. Add pasta and stir to combine.

The mac and cheese can be served at this point or placed in a baking dish, topped with buttered bread crumbs, and baked at 350°F for 30 minutes.

THE YELLOW PORCH

734 THOMPSON LANE, BERRY HILL
(615) 386-0260
THEYELLOWPORCH.COM
CHEF: GUERRY McCOMAS JR.
OWNERS: GEP AND KATIE NELSON

I've spent plenty of time on the porch that gives this cozy Berry Hill location its name, enjoying the herb and flower garden that somehow thrives a few feet from the busy stretch of Thompson Lane. Gep and Katie Nelson's Yellow Porch always seems, like its Brentwood sister Wild Iris, to have distinctly fresh (in all senses of the word) and creative takes on food.

Berry Hill has long been divided by Thompson Lane—there's the big Vanderbilt Health Center to the south that's taken over the old 100 Oaks Mall and revitalized it, and a host of innovative small businesses operating out of tiny '40s and '50s ranch-style homes to the north. The Yellow Porch sits right on the dividing line, serving the patrons of both worlds and all those who drive in as well.

The Yellow Porch gets extra credit for managing paella very well, and the sweet tea–cured smoked pork chop is marvelous. The lunch menu brims with excellent salads, including a very good take on the now-classic Black and Blue Salad, with seared sirloin, blue cheese, tomatoes, crispy onions, and herb ranch dressing, garnished with bacon and cucumber.

The recipe provided here for the cheese fritters is absolutely delicious. It's a perfect starter or appetizer to pass at a party. Chef Guerry McComas makes use of local favorite Sweetwater Valley cheddar cheese, which you can order from the website listed below, or substitute your own favorite sharp cheddar. These recipes are designed to be served together—the chow chow makes a wonderful, spicy contrast to the cheese fritters—and the fritters themselves dip right into the spicy, Sriracha-laced aioli.

TENNESSEE SHARP CHEDDAR CHEESE FRITTERS

(MAKES 16–18 FRITTERS)

1½ pounds Sweetwater Valley cheddar,* shredded

3 cups all-purpose flour

2 teaspoons baking powder

2 cups buttermilk

5 eggs

1 tablespoon Old Bay seasoning

1 tablespoon salt

¼ cup chopped chives

Place all the ingredients in a stand mixer bowl and mix with the paddle attachment until well combined.

Using a 2-ounce scoop or 2 large spoons, scoop out and fry the batter at 350°F for about 4–5 minutes or until each fritter is golden brown.

*Note: You can order Tennessee's Sweetwater Valley cheddar at sweetwatervalley.com, or substitute Cabot (Vermont) sharp white cheddar, available at most grocery stores. Any good locally made sharp white would also be excellent if available, according to Chef Guerry.

CHOW CHOW

(MAKES 2 QUARTS)

1 head green cabbage, shredded
1 yellow onion, small dice
1 red bell pepper, small dice
¼ cup kosher salt
1 quart cider vinegar
2 cups sugar
1 tablespoon dry mustard
1½ teaspoons turmeric
1 teaspoon ground ginger
1 tablespoon mustard seeds
1 teaspoon crushed red pepper

In a bowl, combine the cabbage, onions, bell peppers, and salt. Toss well and let sit for 24 hours.

Combine the vinegar and spices in a sauce pot, bring to a boil, and simmer for 10 minutes.

While the vinegar mixture is coming to a boil, drain the cabbage mix in a colander. Add the cabbage to the vinegar, bring back to a boil, and simmer for 10 more minutes.

Pour the mixture into a container, cover, label, and date. The chow chow can be used as soon as it cools down, however, the flavor will improve over time. It will keep for a month or more in the refrigerator.

SPICY AIOLI

(MAKES 1¼ CUPS, ENOUGH FOR THE FRITTER RECIPE)

1 cup mayonnaise
2 tablespoons Sriracha hot sauce
2 tablespoons Thai sweet chili sauce

Mix all the ingredients together and set aside to serve with the fritters. The aioli can be used right away, or it should keep for at least a couple of weeks in a sealed container in the refrigerator.

Plate the dish with aioli in the middle for dipping the cheese fritters and chow chow to garnish.

Resource Guide

Where to order all those fabulous regional food products

Arnold Myint
Smoked salt and other artisan products
www.arnoldmyint.com

Arrington Vineyards
*Locally produced wines from Williamson County, favorites
include Red Fox Red, Stag's White*
6211 Patton Rd.
Arrington, TN 37014
(615) 395-0102
arringtonvineyards.com

Bang Candy Company
*Artisan marshmallows, candies, and sweets, plus simple
syrups for cocktails and baking*
1300 Clinton St., Suite 127
Nashville, TN 37203
(615) 953-1065
bangcandycompany.com

Benton's Smoky Mountain Country Hams
Bacon, country ham and pork products
2603 Hwy. 411 North
Madisonville, TN 37354-6356
(423) 442-5003
bentonscountryhams2.com

Bongo Java Coffee
Wholesale and retail fair trade coffees
2007 Belmont Blvd.
Nashville, TN 37212
(615) 385-5282
bongojava.com/

Dozen Bakery
*Cakes, pies, cookies, and more; made to order with
organic ingredients*
(615) 509-9680
dozen-nashville.com

Firepot Chai
Hand-blended chai concentrate from fair trade or better ingredients, custom teas
2905 12th Ave. S., Suite 106
Nashville, TN 37204
facebook.com/firepot-chai, firepotchai.com, ThirdWaveTeas.com

Goo Goo Clusters/Standard Candy Company
Tennessee original candies, wholesale and retail
715 Massman Dr.
Nashville, TN 37210
googoo.com

Kenny's Farmhouse Cheese
Artisan cheeses from the region, from Asiago to Swiss, plus gift baskets
2033 Thomerson Park Rd.
Austin, KY 42123
(888) 571-4029
kennysfarmhousecheese.com

Noble Springs Dairy
Goat's milk cheeses and other products
3144 Blazer Rd.
Franklin, TN 37064
(615) 481-9546
noble-springs.com

Olive & Sinclair Chocolates
Bean to bar handmade chocolate, in a variety of flavors
1404 McGavock Pike
Nashville, TN 37216
(615) 262-3007
oliveandsinclair.com

Roast, Inc. (8th & Roast)
Better than fair trade hand-roasted coffees
2108A 8th Ave. South
Nashville, TN 37204
(615) 730-8074
facebook.com/roastinc

Silke's Old World Breads
Fresh, European-style, handmade breads, cakes, and pastries
1214 College St.
Clarksville, TN 37040
silkesoldworldbreads.com

Sunburst Trout Farms
Fresh trout, caviar and other food products
128 Raceway Place
Canton, NC 28716
(828) 648-3010
sunbursttroutfarms.com

Sweetwater Valley Farm
A wide variety of cheeses, including flavored cheddars and cheese curds; farm tours welcome
17988 W. Lee Hwy.
Philadelphia, TN 37846
(865) 458-9192
(877) 862-4332
sweetwatervalley.com

Triple L Ranch
Free range meats, including beef
5121 Bedford Creek Rd.
Franklin, TN 37064
(615) 799-2823
lllranch.com

TruBee Honey
Regional Tennessee raw honeys and honey straws
trubeehoney.com

Whisper Creek Tennessee Sipping Cream
Original cream liquor made in Nashville;, distillery tours available
900 44th Ave. North (SPEAKeasy Spirits campus)
Nashville, TN 37209
tennesseesippingcream.com; buy online at www.binny's.com

Note: Most of the locally based spirits in the book are available nationally through distributors. State laws make it difficult to buy some directly over the Internet. For more information please visit the following sites for products recommended in this book by Nashville mixologists.

Collier & McKeel Tennessee Whiskey
collierandmckeel.com

Corsair Artisan Distillery
corsairartisan.com

George Dickel Tennessee Whiskey
dickel.com

Jack Daniel's Tennessee Whiskey
jackdaniels.com

Nelson's Greenbrier Distillery (Belle Meade Bourbon)
greenbrierdistillery.com

Prichard's Distillery
prichardsdistillery.com

Short Mountain Distillery (Tennessee traditional moonshine)
shortmountaindistillery.com

Woodford Reserve Kentucky Bourbon
woodfordreserve.com

Pork Tenderloin with Peach Salad, Shaved Radicchio & Sweet Cherry Gastrique, 56
Puckett's Chicken Salad, 144
Salad with Fresh Strawberries, Blue Cheese, Toasted Almonds & White Balsamic Vinaigrette, 111
Salad with Green Goddess Dressing, 39
Strawberry Salad, 127
Thai Cobb Salad, 189
Tuna, Eggplant & Spinach Ponzu Salad, 66–67
Salmon
  Smoked Salmon Dressing, 131
  Smoked Salmon with Orecchiette Pasta, 31
Salsas
  Edamame Salsa, 1
Sandwiches
  Grilled Cheese, 89
  Nashville Hot Chicken, 76
  Puckett's King's French Toast, 146
  Pulled Pork with Caraway Slaw & Homemade Dijon Mustard, 164–66
  Ramsey Burger, The, 25
Sauces
  Aioli, 185
  Homemade Dijon Mustard, 166
  Mango Chili Sauce, 26–28
  Pecan Romesco, 124
  Rouille, 185
  Spicy Aioli, 194
Scarborough, Sarah, 78
Schultheis, Carl, 48, 74, 147
Seafood suppliers, 177
Sears, Scott, 82

Shellfish
  BBQ Shrimp, 168
  Bouillabaisse, 184
  Crab Cakes with Asian Slaw & Mango Chili Sauce, 26–28
  King Kong Couscous, 162
  Lobster & Brie "Mac and Cheese" with Benton's Smoky Mountain Country Ham Crisp, 28
  Shrimp & Grits with Pickled Okra, 175
  suppliers of, 177
Shortcakes
  Brown Sugar Shortcakes, 53
Shrimp
  BBQ Shrimp, 168
  Bouillabaisse, 184
  King Kong Couscous, 162
  Shrimp & Grits with Pickled Okra, 175
Shuff, Christy, 150
Side dishes. See also Salads; Soups
  Brussels Sprouts, 22
  Butternut Rotolo, 49
  Carrot Pudding, 101
  Collard Greens, 99
  Double-Fried French Fries, 37
  Mac & Cheese (Arnold's Country Kitchen), 5
  Sautéed Swiss Chard, 39
  Southern Corn Bread, 98
  Southern Green Beans, 5
  Vegetable Frites, 35
Silly Goose, 160–62
Sloco, 163–66
Soups
  Bouillabaisse, 184
  Chicken Tortilla Soup, 121
  Creamy Tomato Basil Soup, 140

Old-Fashioned Tomato Soup, 90
Onion Soup Gratinée, 186
Souther, Sarah, 10
Southern Steak & Oyster, The, 167–70
Speakeasy Spirits, 154
Spinach
  Mini Spinach Feta Frittata, 60
  Tuna, Eggplant & Spinach Ponzu Salad, 66–67
Stephenson, John, 72
Stocks
  Fish Stock, 184
Strawberries
  Salad with Fresh Strawberries, Blue Cheese, Toasted Almonds & White Balsamic Vinaigrette, 111
  Strawberry Salad, 127
Sunset Grill, 172–76
Supper clubs, 104
Swagruha, 178–80
Sweet potatoes
  Double-Fried French Fries, 37
  Sofia's Sweet Potato Truffles, 46
  Sweet Potato Gnocchi with Spiced Parmesan Cream, 86–87
  Sweet Potato Guava Schmear, 65
Swiss chard
  Sautéed Swiss Chard, 39
Syrups
  Basil Grapefruit Syrup, 51

Table 3 Restaurant & Market, 182–86
Tacos
  Redneck Taco, 118
Tardo, Vinny, 156

Tassone, Danny, 142
Tavern, 188–89
Thouin, Bethany, 45
Tomatoes
  Creamy Tomato Basil
    Soup, 140
  Edamame Salsa, 1
  Johnny Cash's "Old Iron Pot"
    Family-Style Chili, 128
  Miss Daisy's Black Bean
    Salad, 134
  Old-Fashioned Tomato
    Soup, 90
  Pecan Romesco, 124
  Tomato Basil Pie, 6
Tomkats, 156, 167
Totzke, Kim, 138
Trout
  Spring Trout, 38

Trucks, food, 18–20, 77, 88–90
Truffles
  Amy's Balsamic Raspberry
    Truffles, 45–46
  Sofia's Sweet Potato
    Truffles, 46
Tuna, Eggplant & Spinach
  Ponzu Salad, 66–67

Uhl, Brian, 26, 130
Uhlhorn, Will, 182

Vegetables
  Vegetable Frites, 35
  Vegetable Korma, 180
Vinaigrettes. *See also*
  Dressings
  Carrot Vinaigrette, 94
  Fish Sauce Vinaigrette, 189

Strawberry Vinaigrette, 127
Tabasco Honey
  Vinaigrette, 173
White Balsamic
  Vinaigrette, 111

Waffles, Pig Ears with, 84
Whiskey Kitchen, 190–91
Wild & Local, 177
Williams, Megan, 62
Williams, Mike, 154
Williamson County, 96
Wilson, Tandy, 42–43
Wood, Brad and Lesa, 59
Worley, Karl, 18

Yazoo Brewery, 154
Yellow Porch, The, 192–94

About the Author & Photographer

Stephanie Stewart-Howard is a journalist and author whose résumé also includes work as an artist, actor, costume designer, and researcher. She received her BA and MA from the Universities of Iowa and Nebraska (Omaha), respectively. After spending several years as managing editor and primary writer at *Nashville Lifestyles* magazine, she decided to leap into the book and freelance world. She has contributed to *Nashville Arts, Cheers!, Sports Nashville,* Volkswagen's *Das Auto, NFocus, The Tennessean, Renaissance* magazine, Liveability.com, and many more publications. She writes regularly on matters of fashion, culinary topics, travel, and the arts. Stephanie was born in Virginia and brought up worldwide thanks to her dad's career in the US Air Force and corporate America. She now resides in an old farmhouse in Williamson County, Tennessee, with her husband, Seth (an IT professional and bladesmith), and their two cats. The couple is active in the medieval and ancient world living-history movements, as well as a variety of arts and crafts.

Ron Manville is a culinary/lifestyle photographer who has photographed sixty-six cookbooks that have garnered seventeen national and international awards, including four James Beards. He is a contributing photographer for *Art Culinare, Grace Ormonde's Wedding Style* magazine, *Local Palate, Nashville Lifestyles,* and many other publications. Ron was Team USA's photographer at two IKA Culinary Olympics competitions in Erfurt, Germany, to highlight a long-term association with the American Culinary Federation. He is a cofounder of Buttermilk Trace, a writer-driven Southern Creative Consortium based in Nashville. He is an RIT graduate and US Navy veteran, and he resides in Nashville with his wife, Christine.

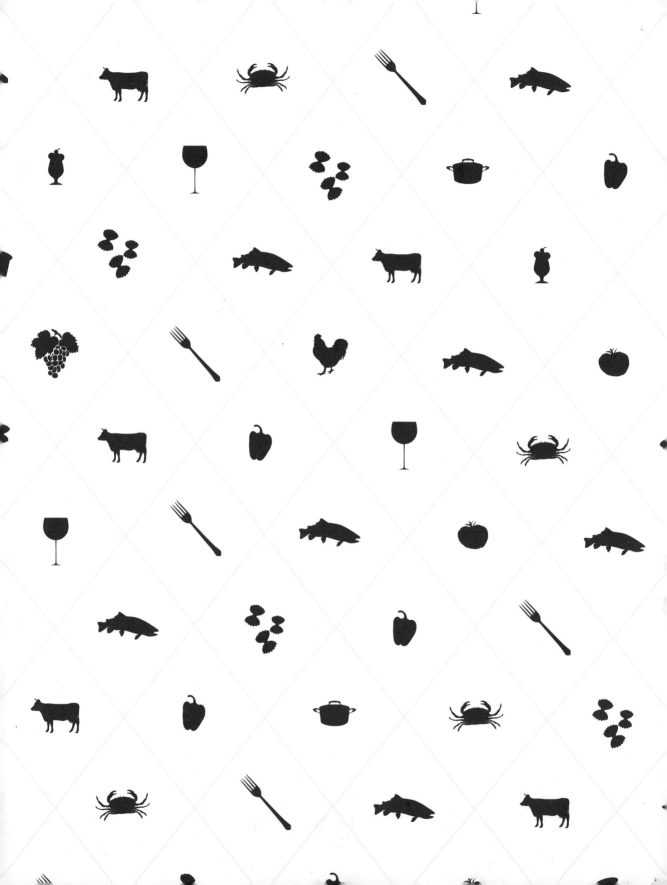